Tom Kusch

Diary of a Unicorn

A Memoir

ISBN 979-8-9934039-1-5 (Paperback)
ISBN 979-8-9934039-0-8 (eBook)
ISBN 979-8-9934039-2-2 (Audiobook)

First Edition: February 2026

Cover design by César Pardo

Printed in the United States of America

For more information or to contact the author, visit:
TomKusch.com

DISCLAIMER

This memoir reflects the author's present recollections of experiences over time. Some names and identifying characteristics have been changed to protect the privacy of individuals. Some events have been compressed, and some dialogue has been recreated from memory.

This book describes the author's experiences and reflects the author's opinions. The views expressed are solely those of the author and should not be attributed to any individuals, companies, or organizations mentioned or implied herein.

While the author has made every effort to provide accurate information and portray events as faithfully as memory allows, no warranty or guarantee is made regarding the accuracy or completeness of the information contained herein.

Table of Contents

PREFACE:
THE BLONDIN MOMENT

You ever notice how people say they believe in you… but when it's time to show it? Crickets.

Back in 1859, Charles Blondin walked across Niagara Falls on a rope. Absolute daredevil. No net. No second chances. Just balance and brass.

He didn't just walk it once. He did it blindfolded, pushing a wheelbarrow, even on stilts. At one point? He stopped mid-rope, sat down… and pulled out a flask of whiskey and drank it. No joke.

The crowd ate it up.

Then one day, he says: "Do you believe I can carry a man across in this wheelbarrow?" Everyone's shouting: "YES!"

So he goes: "Cool. Who's coming with me?"

Silence.

Look, life's risky. There's never a perfect moment. Sometimes, you gotta be the one who says:

"Put me in the wheelbarrow. Let's go."

This book is what happened when I started getting in the wheelbarrow. Sometimes I carried people. Sometimes they carried me. Sometimes I fell off.

Here's what I remember.

PROLOGUE:
THE SECURITY GUARD

The bass line from the opening band was still vibrating through the concrete floor when I had no idea how I'd gotten here. It's New Year's Eve, 2011, and I'm standing at the edge of the stage at the Joe Louis Arena in Detroit, wearing a bright yellow security t-shirt that's too big for me and a radio clipped to my belt that keeps crackling with urgent-sounding codes I don't understand. The arena holds 20,000 people, and it feels like every single one of them is here tonight, pressed against the barriers, waiting for the Zac Brown Band to take the stage.

I have foam earplugs stuffed deep in my ears, but I'm not here to see the show. I am a security guard. The guy who spent his childhood breaking rules and sneaking into places he wasn't supposed to be is now the one enforcing them.

Six hours earlier, I'd been sitting in my apartment, staring at a bank account that was barely breathing and a stack of bills that seemed to multiply every time I looked away. A friend had called with this gig. I said no. He said it's easy money, stand there and look official. I needed the cash, so I finally said yes without thinking about what "security" would mean.

Now, standing in the amber glow of the stage lights, watching the crowd surge and sway like a living thing, I'm thinking to myself, this was not on my plate for something to do this morning, let alone in my lifetime. But there I am, game face on, trying to project an authority I definitely don't feel.

The Zac Brown Band hasn't started yet, so I strike up a conversation with the fans closest to the stage. They're friendly: a mix of couples on date nights, groups of friends celebrating, and die-hard fans who've been waiting here since the doors opened. One woman is wearing a homemade t-shirt with the band's lyrics scrawled in glitter pen. A guy next to her keeps checking his phone, taking pictures of the empty stage. The energy is electric, anticipatory. This might be a good night.

Then, about twenty feet to my left, a fight breaks out.

At first, I pretend I can't see it. I look the other way, suddenly very interested in the rigging high above the stage. Maybe it'll resolve itself. Maybe they'll walk away from each other. Maybe someone else will handle it.

But the woman with the glitter shirt tugs on my sleeve. "Hey, security guy," she says, pointing toward the scuffle. "You better get over there."

My stomach drops. The radio on my hip crackles again, voices calling out positions and updates in that clipped, professional tone that makes everything sound urgent. I scan the crowd for backup, for one of the veteran guards who knows what they're doing, but everyone else is either too far away or dealing with their own situations.

I take a deep breath, feeling my heart start to pound against my ribs, and work my way through the crowd. People step aside as they see the yellow shirt coming, creating a narrow path through the press of bodies. The smell hits me as I move: beer, perfume, sweat, and that particular scent of excitement that comes off a crowd this size.

When I reach the disturbance, I see it's a man and a woman, both probably in their thirties, yelling at each other with the kind of fury that suggests this isn't their first fight. They're not throwing punches, but they're in each other's faces, voices raised over the ambient noise of 20,000 people. From what I can piece together, they bumped into each other trying to get closer to the stage, and it escalated from there.

"You pushed me!" she's shouting.

"I didn't push anybody!" he shouts back. "You were in my way!"

The people around them have formed a loose circle, some filming with their flip phones, others watching with the fascination people have for conflict that isn't theirs. The man is bigger, louder, and clearly intoxicated. The woman is holding her ground but looks like she's about to either cry or throw a punch.

I step between them, my voice finding a calm, projected tone I didn't know I had. "Hey, folks. May I remind you that you are at a concert on the floor." I gesture to the crowd around us, the stage, the anticipation hanging in the air. "There will be bumping. It's going to happen all night. Why don't you separate and enjoy the show? Because if I have to come back over here, I won't be alone, and the people who come with me will kick you out. I don't want to start your new year off that way."

They both look at me, then at each other. For a moment, I think it might escalate further. The man's jaw is clenched, his hands balled into fists. The woman has tears of frustration in her eyes. The crowd around us holds its breath.

Then something shifts. Maybe it's the reasonableness in my voice, or maybe they realize how ridiculous they look fighting over a few square feet of concrete. The man shakes his head and walks away, muttering under his breath. The woman wipes her eyes and turns back toward the stage.

The crowd disperses, the crisis passes, and I walk back to my post near the barrier. My hands are shaking slightly from the adrenaline.

As I settle back into position, the woman with the glitter shirt catches my eye and gives me a thumbs up. "Nice job, security guy," she says with a grin.

The Zac Brown Band takes the stage a few minutes later, and the arena erupts. The bass line that had been rumbling through the building all evening gives way to the opening chords of their first song, and 20,000 people become one voice, singing along to every word. I stand there in my too-big yellow shirt, foam plugs still in my ears, and watch this massive celebration unfold in front of me.

PART ONE:
THE WANDERER'S ROOTS

E very house has its rules. Every kid finds the loopholes.
These are the years before anyone handed me a badge or
a business card. Before the cubicles and the commutes. Back
when the biggest question was whether figs were made of bugs
and the most important skill was knowing when to flip a burger.

Something was different about the way I saw things. I just
didn't have a name for it yet.

1-1:
THE WALLET IN THE WALL
(1988)

The little girl from across the street showed up at my door. She wanted me to come over and play.

I told her I couldn't cross the street without an adult.

"I'm older than you," she said. "I'm allowed to. If I hold your hand, that counts."

A hand was a hand. Made sense to me.

We looked both ways, held hands, and crossed the street together. Both of us completely sure we'd figured out a loophole in the rules.

My mom was watching from our front window. She came outside, trying not to laugh. She wasn't mad, but she did explain that when they said "adult," they meant someone a lot older than six.

Her house was different. Messy. Not kid mess. Stuff everywhere that nobody picked up. Dishes in the sink for days. The

TV was on loud in the living room, but her mom wasn't watching it. It was on. Making noise.

The garage leaned to one side like it was tired.

I was four. I didn't think it was weird. It was her house.

Her mom was there, but she didn't look at us much. My mom was always asking questions, always watching what we were doing. Her mom walked around like she was thinking about something else.

My mom always made sure the kids on our block had food.

On this particular day, my friend and I were playing with her dolls on the floor of her living room. We were making up stories, the way kids do, completely absorbed in the game.

Then her mom came through. She looked at us, and her face changed. Got harder. Like we were in her way and she was annoyed about it.

I'd never seen a mom look at a kid like that.

My friend's face got mean looking.

She walked over to a nearby table where her mom's wallet sat with some other stuff.

I wasn't paying attention at first. One of the kids from down the street had given us Fig Newtons earlier, and I was still trying to figure out if figs were made of bugs like someone had told me. That seemed important to figure out.

My friend opened the wallet. Inside were the colorful plastic cards my parents had too. I recognized the Mastercard logo, the Visa symbol. And some green money folded up.

Then she walked over to this big hole in the wall where a vent cover should have been. You could see right into the dark metal ductwork behind the wall.

She held the wallet over the hole and started dropping things in. One card. Then another. The cards made a little metallic clink as they hit the metal inside. Then the money. It didn't fall straight like the cards did. It floated and spun before disappearing into the dark.

I was still thinking about the Fig Newtons. Were figs bugs or not? I couldn't figure it out.

"Mommy will be looking for this for a while," she said. Her voice sounded happy, but also not happy.

When the wallet was empty, she closed it and put it back exactly where she'd found it, like nothing had happened.

Then she came back over, picked up her doll, and we ... played. Like normal. Like she hadn't thrown all her mom's stuff into the wall.

It felt bad. Like when you see something you're not supposed to see.

I wanted to tell my mom. But I didn't.

So I kept playing with the dolls and didn't say anything.

We stopped playing together after that.

1-2:
THE MOVE
(1989)

I was four years old when the monster attacked our lawn.

I was in the living room of our little bungalow in Detroit, playing with my favorite toy. A van that was also a tent, made of sturdy plastic walls stretched over a metal frame. That new plastic smell that got hot and heavy in the Detroit summer. My brother, who was only two, was nearby with his own collection of toys.

Then, from somewhere outside, I heard a sound. It didn't sound like anything I'd heard before. It was scary. A slow, mechanical coughing, like something large trying to wake up from a long sleep.

The sound started with a pull and a sputter. Zip hiss sputter. Silence. Another pull, another mechanical cough. Each attempt sounded more violent than the last, as if whatever was making the noise was getting angrier. Then, with a sound that seemed to shake the foundations of our small house, the thing roared to life. A sharp, hot smell filled the air.

To my four-year-old brain, completely unfamiliar with the routine sounds of lawn maintenance, this wasn't yard work. This was a monster.

I looked at my brother. He's always been fine with loud noises. Even at two, he was probably continuing to play, completely unbothered. But his calm didn't matter to me. Whether he understood the danger or not, it was my job to keep him safe.

I grabbed his hand and made a decision that felt like the most important decision I had ever made. Get to safety. And in my kid brain, safety was always up.

The stairs were normally forbidden territory. One of the cardinal rules of our household. But there was a monster outside, and the normal rules no longer applied. We crawled up those stairs together, my brother following my lead.

When we reached the top, we made our way to the big room. Our parents' bedroom. We found our hiding spot behind the bed. The floor was covered with a super-fuzzy, baby blue rug that looked handmade, probably created by one of our grandmothers. We huddled together on that soft surface, waiting for the monster to go away.

The roaring seemed to last forever. Then, as mysteriously as it had begun, it stopped. The silence that followed was huge and significant.

Eventually, when we felt safe enough, we made our way back downstairs and returned to our toys as if nothing extraordinary had happened.

Turns out the "monster" was my dad mowing the lawn.

That house, that little bungalow where monsters could attack at any moment and stairs were forbidden adventures, was the only home my brother and I had ever known. Which is why, when I was five and my brother was three, the announcement came as such a surprise.

I don't remember my parents sitting us down for a formal family meeting. What I remember is boxes appearing. Big cardboard boxes. I loved big boxes. You could play in them, hide in them, build forts with them.

But then things started disappearing into those boxes. The mirror on the wall. 12 by 12 mirrored tiles with black and white grids silk screened on the frame. I thought that was permanent, part of the house itself. Watching it come down and get wrapped up was strange. Made the space look so different for little kid me. Everything I thought was a fixture was being packed away.

One day, our little bungalow was our entire universe, and the next day, that familiar world was being taken apart.

My most vivid memory of the moving process isn't of packing or watching our belongings disappear into a truck. It's of people.

The entire ski club showed up in full force. The morning was a blur of pickup trucks and familiar faces.

The group was full of the same characters who defined all of our social gatherings. There was my dad's friend, the engineering type who fixed assembly lines for an automotive company and seemed to own every tool ever invented. He'd brought his pickup truck loaded with moving supplies and, most impressively, a special winch device he'd built specifi-cally for moving heavy objects up and down stairs. This wasn't something you could buy at a hardware store. It was a custom solution, and watching him deploy it on our heaviest furniture was like watching a master craftsman with a tool designed for exactly this purpose.

Another friend had brought his Corvette, as he did to every gathering, making his usual announcement that he didn't want to carry anything heavy in his pristine sports car but was happy to provide moral support and supervisory assistance. This was a running joke within the group. A vehicle completely impracti-cal for any actual work, combined with his willingness to con-tribute in every way that didn't involve risking damage to his automotive pride and joy.

But the real dynamo of the operation was the small, unstoppable woman everyone called "the old poop." She never stopped moving throughout the entire day, carrying boxes, organizing supplies, directing traffic, and generally functioning as the unofficial coordinator who made sure nothing was for-gotten or overlooked.

Amidst all this adult activity, my brother and I had our own separate adventures. I was fascinated by the moving dolly and kept stealing it from the adults. Someone had the genius idea to solve this problem by convincing me to trade the dolly for my Big Wheel. A transaction that seemed perfectly reason-able to my five-year-old sensibilities.

The Big Wheel was my primary vehicle for neighborhood exploration, a low-riding tricycle with gray plastic frame and bright blue handlebars. My brother had his own beloved vehicle. A little blue truck with a yellow handle. We would chase each other at top speeds down the sidewalks.

I was in the moving truck with my dad, chattering away with endless questions about how the stick shift worked. True to form, he kept asking me to explain it, even though he obviously knew. He knew that my aunt would let me shift her car's gears for her during our rides, and while I wasn't shifting the truck, I would earnestly tell him when it was time to change gears. I didn't know what RPMs were, but I knew the sound. The engine getting higher and strained. That was the tell. Time to shift.

He humored me every single time, treating my technical advice with serious consideration. This became one of my earliest and most cherished memories. Not the novelty of riding in a big truck, but how much fun it was to have my dad treat my observations as genuinely valuable.

The new house was bigger. More rooms, more space. The lot was bigger, providing more outdoor space. The roads were smoother. Everything felt newer, cleaner.

It was an open house when we first got there. I ran through it, room to room. My Big Wheel was easy to get off the moving truck, and they handed it to me pretty quick. Probably to get me out of the way.

The big glass door wall in the back had a view of the woods. That's what got me. It was very green. Went on as far as I could see. Those woods would become a primary playground as we got older.

My brother and I explored together.

A few years later, when I was about nine and my brother was seven, we spent most of our time in those woods. My brother and

I always had each other's backs out there, especially in the woods. Our biggest fear wasn't an animal. It was another person, another kid invading our territory. We found them soon enough. A rival group with their own fort. At first, we were all scared of each other, crafting swords out of sticks for the kind of make-believe fights that felt deadly serious at the time.

But eventually, the rivalry gave way to an alliance. Our forts merged, and we became a single tribe of explorers. It was during one of our joint scavenging missions that we found the treasure. A giant Coca-Cola bottle bank. The 2 foot tall kind. Thick, translucent green plastic with a red screw on cap.

Through the plastic you could see the layers. The dull brown of the copper pennies. The flashes of silver from the nickels and quarters. The way the coins settled into the five bumped star shape base of the bottle.

It was so heavy it took two of us to carry it back. When we brought it home to my dad, he picked it up with one arm like it was nothing while we had struggled to carry it together. That bottle was a heavy, sloshing anchor. Had to weigh 40 to 70 pounds. We had to take it to the police station and file a report.

The police station was a low slung tan brick building. The front doors were heavy. Commercial grade glass and metal that hissed when they closed behind you, cutting off the noise of the traffic outside.

Inside smelled like floor wax, coffee, and stale cigarette smoke that had been baked into the ceiling tiles for twenty years. Harsh, flickering lights that buzzed overhead.

The lobby had a high counter. At nine years old, I had to stand on my tiptoes. My dad helped me hoist the bottle onto the ledge.

My dad stood behind me with a hand on my shoulder. He didn't do the talking. He made me explain it.

Where I found it. The woods. What it was. The Coke bottle bank. That we wanted to turn it in.

The officer wore a dark navy blue uniform. A heavy leather duty belt with all his gear on it.

I pushed that massive, coin filled bottle across the counter toward him. The scrape of plastic on the counter. The sound of our treasure leaving our hands for 30 days.

The officer filled out a Found Property report on a standard clipboard. Asked for my name and address. He gave me a yellow carbon copy receipt. The legal proof that if no one claimed the Monster Bottle in 30 days, it was ours. I held onto that receipt like it was the golden ticket.

Those thirty days were torture. We'd gather with the other kids, spread out the Funcoland newspaper and dream. Funcoland was this video game store where you could buy used games. They had this newspaper. A yellow off white newsprint flyer with tiny 8 point font. It listed every game with Buy prices and Sell prices.

We weren't just dreaming. We were doing math. Calculating how to maximize that bottle's value. A used copy of Super Mario World or The Legend of Zelda A Link to the Past might be $25 to $30. Older NES games like Top Gun or Operation Wolf could be as little as 49 cents to $1.99. We'd calculate how many old games we had to trade in to get that one treasure game. If there was $60 in that bottle, we weren't just getting a game. We were getting an entire library.

It was one of the first places our parents let us walk to from the house. We counted the money in the jug, calculated how to split it, and planned our future purchases down to the last cent.

Thirty days later we walked back into that station. The officer slid that bottle back to us. This time for keeps.

Walking back out into the bright sun, feeling like kings. We bought the video games we'd spent a month obsessing over.

1-3:
THE SOUND OF SUMMER SHATTERING

(1991)

The suburbs were quiet. Manicured lawns. The gentle hum of central air conditioning. Kids playing in sprinklers.

The day it happened wasn't dark or stormy. The weather was phenomenally beautiful. One of those perfect Michigan summer days that arrive like an unexpected gift. The sky stretched overhead in a deep, cloudless blue. The air was warm but not oppressive. Carrying the sweet, green scent of freshly cut grass and the distant aroma of someone's barbecue starting up early.

Our house sat in the heart of suburban Detroit. A brick ranch built in the 1950s that my parents had bought when they decided the city wasn't the place to raise two boys. The sliding glass door had been added in the 1960s. The neighborhood was the kind where kids could still ride their bikes in the street. Where everyone knew which dog would bark at you through the fence but never bite. Where you could walk to the ice cream shop on the corner for a cone on hot summer days.

I had a very clear logic as a kid. When my dad moved his minivan from the driveway to the garage in the morning, I would move my bike from the garage to the driveway. It was a perfect system in my eight-year-old mind. The minivan needed the driveway space to back out safely. My bike needed a place to live where I could grab it at a moment's notice for adventure. Later in the day, when he reversed the process and moved the minivan back to the driveway, I'd move my bike back to its home in the garage. It was a perfect, silent partnership. A small ritual in the rhythm of our suburban Detroit life that made me feel important.

The bike itself was my pride and joy. A black frame with bright red handlebar grips. My dad was good at teaching us to oil our bikes every spring. We knew how to use the air pump to fill the tires. Made sure we knew how to take care of them.

I was just about to move my bike when I saw the mail carrier making their way down the block. She was a beast of a woman. Not in any negative sense, but in the way that suggests someone built for hard work and endurance. She had been our mail carrier for as long as I could remember. Graying hair pulled back in a practical ponytail and a smile that never seemed forced, even on the hottest days. She walked with purpose. Her blue uniform crisp despite the heat. Her bag slung across her shoulder with the confidence of someone who had walked these same streets for decades.

Filled with the excitement only a kid can feel for something as mundane as the daily mail delivery, I abandoned my bike-moving mission and ran to the front yard. There was always the possibility of something wonderful arriving. A magazine. A letter from a distant relative. Even just a colorful advertisement that seemed magical to young eyes.

I ran across the yard in my sneakers. My parents had strict rules about shoes.

The mail, when it arrived, was the usual collection of adult mysteries. Bills. Advertisements. A few catalogs. But to me, it was a collection of important documents that needed immediate attention.

That's when my brother and I started fighting. We fought a lot. We also played together a lot. It was weird.

I don't know why we did it. We just did. We each had a big red button. A specific trigger that we knew exactly how to push with surgical precision.

The big rule was: You could never tell the other one what to do. It was an unwritten law that governed our interactions. We could suggest. We could cajole. We could even bribe. But we could never command.

I had the mail clutched in my small fists. Looking at my brother, I made the fatal error. "Take this inside," I said.

He turned and ran toward the house. The door. I sprinted after him, but he was faster. I reached the sliding glass door as he slammed it shut. Through the glass, I could still see him on the other side, lit up with the pure joy of victory, as he dropped the security bar into the track.

He had won, and we both knew it.

I was so mad. Madder than I'd ever been.

So I kicked the door.

Then I kicked it again, harder. And again, each impact more desperate than the last as the rage built inside me.

It took several kicks before the glass finally gave way.

The sound.

That sharp, explosive crack that ripped through the calm afternoon air. Loud enough to bring my dad running from wherever he'd been in the house.

My dad had been in the living room. Settled into his favorite chair with the Sunday newspaper spread across his lap. The sound of exploding glass cut through his peaceful afternoon like a fire alarm.

This wasn't modern, tempered glass that crumbles into safe small cubes. This was old glass from the 1960s. It blew apart in giant, dangerous shards that scattered across the patio. The shattered glass sparkled in the afternoon light. It shone like the blade of a knife. I knew immediately how sharp it was and that I didn't want anything to do with it.

The rage vanished instantly.

The crack. Then silence. Heavy, telling silence.

Then I felt really bad. Like I was in big trouble.

Through the gaping hole, I saw my brother's face flash genuine concern for a split second. Then survival instincts kicked in. He vanished into the house, leaving me to face the music alone.

My dad appeared in the doorway a few moments later, still holding a section of the newspaper. He looked at the shattered glass, then at me.

He was stern, but there was no anger behind it, no shouting. "Go to your room," was all he said.

I was the only one in trouble, and that felt profoundly lonely. My brother was already there when I arrived, sitting on the bottom bunk. He didn't say anything. Didn't gloat, didn't apologize. He sat there.

That's why "Take this inside" set him off.

Later that afternoon, I found myself in my favorite hiding place. The bay window in the living room. It was a beautiful stained-wood alcove with five large windows that looked out over our front yard. On normal days, it was my command center. But today, I was waiting for the repairman.

I wasn't sad. I was excited. I loved work vans.

When the repairman arrived, his vehicle was everything I had hoped it would be. A big white van with a ladder on the roof rack and special metal racks along the side holding large sheets of glass, each one secured with rubber padding and straps.

The repairman himself had the unhurried confidence of someone who had been doing this job for decades. He didn't seem surprised by what he saw. Just another piece of glass to replace.

The process of removing the broken glass was fascinating. He used huge suction cups to grip the remaining shards and lift them safely out of the frame. It was a feat of strength and skill that amazed me. The way he could maneuver these heavy, dangerous pieces of glass with such precision.

But the real magic happened when he started to cut the replacement glass.

I had read The Great Brain books in school. One of them had this trick where a kid soaked a string in lighter fluid, tied it around a bottle, lit it, and dunked it in cold water to make a clean break. But this man used proper tools. A glass cutter with a small, sharp wheel and a straight edge to guide it.

The sound was unforgettable. A horrible screeching noise that made your teeth hurt, like fingernails on a chalkboard amplified. He ran the tool along his measured line, scoring the glass with patient, careful strokes. Then he placed his hands on either side of the scored line and applied pressure. With a sharp, satisfying snap, the glass broke free along the line, as clean and straight as if it had been cut by a machine.

It fit on the first try.

Within an hour of his arrival, we had a brand new sliding glass door, like nothing happened. The only evidence was the small pile of broken glass he loaded into his van and took away.

That night at dinner, my parents instituted a new rule. When we were angry with each other, we had to take ten deep breaths and count to ten before we could react.

It seemed simple.

My brother and I looked at each other across the table. He nodded. So did I.

1-4:
THE UNOFFICIAL RULES OF ENGAGEMENT

(1992)

If my brother and I were adversaries in the Battle of the Sliding Glass Door, we were allies in a much more important campaign: pranking Mom.

We learned from the best. My family functioned on banter. It was how we showed affection and kept each other sharp. My dad had this incredible gift for quick wit and perfect timing, especially when it came to my mom's questions about dinner plans. She'd ask where we should go eat, and he'd rattle off every restaurant that had ever existed in our city, including the ones that had been closed for decades, delivered with the enthusiasm of someone providing genuinely helpful suggestions.

My aunt brought her own brand of mischief to the mix. One Saturday afternoon when my mom needed to make a quick trip to the bank, my aunt saw an opportunity.

The bank had an ATM built directly into the exterior wall. Green screen with blocky text. My mom walked up to the machine while my aunt stayed behind the wheel.

As my mom got out and headed for the ATM, my aunt's grin should have been a warning to anyone paying attention.

It was exciting. Conspiratorial. Fun to be my aunt's accomplice. This obviously wasn't the first time she'd messed with her sister.

The timing had to be perfect. My aunt waited until my mom was fully engaged with the ATM, her back turned to the van. Then she put the van in gear and drove it around the corner of the building, completely out of sight.

When my mom finished her transaction and turned around, there was an empty parking space.

She stood there with a look of genuine confusion, her head turning left and right. You could almost see the gears turning: I know I parked right here. The van was right here thirty seconds ago.

From our hiding spot around the corner, we had a perfect view of her bewilderment. She walked to where the van had been, looked around the parking lot as if a minivan might be hiding behind a compact car, and then stood there with her hands on her hips.

When my mom's confusion was starting to turn into genuine concern, my aunt drove the van back around the corner. The moment my mom saw the car had moved, with her still-warm driver's seat now occupied by a grinning aunt, her face went through confusion, realization, and then genuine laughter. She shook her head and got back in the passenger seat, laughing despite herself.

My aunt knew when to stop.

The pranks were a constant reset back to us being us. Anything that was on her mind was gone.

Bowling nights were special. Dad would make pierogi and kielbasa, and we'd watch James Bond movies together. So when I decided to hide under the bed, I wasn't pranking Mom. I was on a mission.

My childhood masterpiece was what I called the Bowling Night Ambush.

Friday night meant bowling league. I knew her routine well enough. She'd move from the bathroom to her bedroom to work on her hair at the mirror. I saw my opportunity maybe an hour before she started getting ready and decided to take my chance.

The setup was simple because it had to be. I had maybe an hour to clear some space under her bed and get into position. The physical challenge of fitting under there was significant for an eight-year-old, but I was determined to pull this off.

It was dusty under there. The air smelled like dust. All I could see was wrapping paper rolls in a clear tote. I waited.

And waited. Lost track of time. Couldn't risk exposing my location. Had to make sure I didn't sneeze.

She came into her room and started getting ready. Put her earrings in. Then the curling iron.

I could smell her hair as she used the curling iron. That slight sizzle. I knew it was hot. Had to wait for her to set it down. The sound of the hot curling iron touching the counter would be my cue.

When she finally set the curling iron on the dresser, I reached out and grabbed her ankle.

The scream that followed was everything I had hoped for. Loud, sharp, and absolutely genuine.

I laughed. Then I saw how scared she was and hugged her.

1-5:
THE LAMINATED SHEET
(1995)

There was a laminated sheet that hung by a thumbtack on our kitchen bulletin board, near the phone mounted on the wall. It was printed on lime green paper with black text. At the top was their logo. A Playboy bunny on skis.

This was the ski club roster. Every member's home and work phone numbers, organized for quick reference.

My parents and their friends were, at various times, a ski club, a golf club, and ultimately, a group of people from all over Metro Detroit who chose to be a family together.

By the phone, my mom kept a separate list. Her work number, my dad's work number, my aunt's work and home numbers. Emergency contacts. The laminated sheet was different. It was everyone.

The heart of this community was the park cookouts. Once a year, a huge cookout at a county park. People paid a couple bucks to cover their food and drinks.

The park had soccer fields and baseball diamonds. A basketball court. A big picnic pavilion that could fit 100 people. A playground with slides and swings. Shaded picnic areas and open green spaces. Walking trails that ran along a branch of the Rouge River.

On one side of our pavilion stretched wooded trails thick with mature trees. My brother and I would disappear into these woods for hours, always on the hunt for "good sticks." A category that was always immediately recognizable when you found the perfect specimen. We'd often gift our best discoveries to the dogs that accompanied their families, watching their pure joy at receiving a particularly excellent stick.

But the true centerpiece was always the grilling operation. The setup involved multiple grills of different sizes, each designed for specific purposes. The real showpiece was a charcoal pit, roughly the size of half a pallet, built from heavy metal mesh and thick grating. This wasn't equipment you could buy at a hardware store. Someone built it.

The operation was run by one of my parents' friends, a man who cooked for a living at a school cafeteria. He was fascinating to watch. He could do many things at once with ease.

The smell was always charcoal. No matter the park or the event, that was the one constant. That, and the sharp scent of lighter fluid as the fire was first getting started, a signal for us kids to stay clear. As a kid, my main goal was to identify the foods that didn't have anything green in them.

The only other constant was the volleyball net. We kids could play until we heard the adults yell, "Volleyball!" That was our cue to scatter, because the game was about to get very intense.

A weathered nylon net held up by yellow or orange nylon ropes staked into the grass with heavy metal spikes. The lines were often just worn patches in the grass or a few strategically placed coolers. Arguments over whether a ball was "in" or "out" were the primary soundtrack to the late afternoon.

The rhythmic hollow thud of the ball hitting the grass would suddenly be replaced by a sharp, stinging smack as someone went for a spike. These were the same people who ten minutes earlier were laughing by the coolers. Now they were diving into the dirt, skinning knees and shouting. High stakes competition for bragging rights that would last until the next cookout.

As soon as you heard the first aggressive "Mine!" or "In!" you knew the pavilion was about to get loud. That was the signal that the adults weren't parents for the next hour. They were athletes.

We'd watch for a while, then get bored and disappear into the nearby woods, the sounds of their game fading behind us.

For years, my role was simple. Be a kid. Play, explore, stay out of trouble, show up when the food was ready.

Then one hot, sunny afternoon, everything changed. The head chef called me over and handed me a spatula and a pair of tongs. My aunt provided the finishing touch. Tall, white paper chef's hats for me and my brother.

I was excited. No longer bored.

Before I could begin, I had to complete the most important ritual in all of professional cooking. The mandatory tong test.

You must click them twice to make sure they work properly. The sound, clack clack, was my official induction into the fraternity of people who cook for other people.

The instruction was straightforward. Flip the meat once, maybe twice if you're adding cheese. Watch for the juices to run clear. The secret to a perfect burger was good cheese and the discipline to resist the urge to constantly flip and poke.

That became my job from then on. The heat was immense, especially during peak summer. The smell of charcoal became a permanent part of my summer wardrobe. But I loved every minute of it.

As the afternoon wore on, the head chef left me in charge. I took over the entire operation. My brother was often right there with me, the two of us working together to keep the food flowing.

Feeding our entire chosen family was genuinely the best job in the world. People would come up, I'd hand them a burger, they'd say thank you. Immediate. Simple.

The view of the party changed completely once I was stationed behind the grill. Everyone came to me. I didn't have to go to them to say hello anymore. I could see the entire gathering. Front row seat to the volleyball game. The sweat on their faces, the dust kicking up. After a set the players would descend on the coolers. The hiss of soda cans opening and the heavy clunk of the plastic lid dropping back onto the ice.

I flipped a burger. Watched the juices. Everyone talking and laughing. My brother next to me doing the same thing.

1-6:
THE HANDS-ON LEARNER
(1995)

My bicycle siren broke again. It was a little yellow speaker, like a tiny PA system for kids. You could amplify your voice or flip a dial for different sound effects: police siren, fire truck horn, ambulance wail, even a wolf howl.

The problem was the battery connector. Thin wires and cheap plastic. It kept breaking.

The first few times, I brought it to my dad. He'd fix it on the dining room table with his soldering iron. I'd watch. The heat, the way the solder melted and hardened to make the connection work again.

One day it broke again. I was tired of waiting. I'd watched him do it enough times. I grabbed the tools and set up on the table.

You have to heat it long enough for the solder to flow, but not so long you damage stuff. You have to hold the small parts steady while using the iron and the solder wire.

When I finished and tested it, the siren worked. I'd fixed it myself. I was so excited.

I loved that bike siren. I had a police scanner too. I'd listen to it and daydream. I even added a strobe light to my bike. Took it off a life jacket and mounted it on.

My dad let us use his tools. He made sure we wore safety glasses. He was always watching but played it loose. Let us attempt things. Established guardrails. Calculated, safe failure.

Most projects were scrap wood and whatever we could imagine.

After fixing the bike siren, I started trying bigger projects. Some went wrong.

The worst was the TV. The one my brother and I used for video games. A small color set in our bedroom. The coax connector on the back was broken.

I thought I could fix it. I'd fixed the bike siren a bunch of times. I'd watched my dad work on stuff. I felt like I understood how electronics worked.

What I didn't know was that TVs store electricity even after you unplug them.

The moment my screwdriver touched the wrong part, loud crack. Flash of light.

That smell. Smoke and electrical fire. Pretty ratchet. That horrible smell that confirmed the failure.

The TV was way more broken now.

My brother was watching. He held his laugh for a second to make sure I was okay. Then burst out laughing. His silence first, checking I was okay, confirmed our pact was still intact. As long as I was okay, we could move on. The shared goal was now covering up the mistake.

We put the back cover on quick and decided not to mention it. The TV was already broken. I made it worse.

After the shock wore off, it was hilarious. The TV didn't work the way I thought it did.

My brother always checked I was okay first. That was his thing. We didn't talk about what to tell our parents. We had this rule: we didn't tattle on each other. We were a team, especially for hiding our mistakes.

There was the time a wrestling match went too far and one of us went through the drywall in our room. We put a poster over the hole before our parents found it. Stayed like that for years until they went out of town one weekend. We were older by then. We figured out how to fix it ourselves.

The biggest project was when my parents started leaving us home alone for short periods. Most kids would watch TV or play games. I saw a chance to do something way cooler.

My brother and I decided to install our own phone line. The plan was to use those AOL free trial disks. America Online sent them in the mail constantly. Temporary access without monthly costs. We ran a complete telephone line from a new outlet we put in our computer room wall, through the house, to the main telephone box.

The installation became a top-secret mission. Brief windows when we were home alone. We used hand drills and hand tools for the whole thing. Power tools would be too loud.

For the final connections to the main telephone box, I looked at what was working for the other outlets in the house and reverse engineered it. Figured it out from seeing how it was already done.

We tested it with another phone before cleaning everything up. It worked. We felt accomplished. Then we put that phone back like we never touched it.

For about a month, we'd dial into the free trials when mom and dad weren't home. We'd get home from school and have a few hours before they got home from work.

They caught on because we ran up the phone bill. We got the area code wrong when we set it up, which meant our connections were long-distance calls. That's what gave it away.

When they found out what we'd done, I laughed. They were more amazed at what we'd pulled off than mad about the cost.

1-7:
THE UNOFFICIAL CONSULTANT
(1990-1996)

My aunt's van was a masterpiece of 1990s excess. Big conversion van. Captain's chairs. Windows with blinds. Rope lights built into the wood grain paneling.

I sat in one of those captain's chairs on Saturday mornings when she'd take me to her office in downtown Detroit. From my window, I watched the city get closer. Buildings getting taller. More glass. More steel.

The office building was a high-rise. Maybe 30 stories. My aunt worked on the 15th floor. Halfway up. All glass and steel on the outside. That meant we got to use the express elevator.

My aunt pulled into the parking structure. We got out. Walked through the marble lobby.

"You have to sneak by security," she said.

I loved that she said it like that. Made me feel like James Bond sneaking past security on a secret mission.

The security desk sat in the middle of the lobby. Two guards. One older, one younger. Both big guys. My aunt knew them. She walked straight through with a little wave.

The younger guard looked up. Saw me. Winked. He was in on it. My aunt was just showing an excited kid around, and he thought it was fun to play along.

Mission accomplished.

The elevators were express. They didn't stop at every floor. They rocketed from the lobby straight to the upper floors. My stomach dropped the first time. The kind of drop that makes you giggle. I giggled every time after that too.

The doors opened on the 15th floor. Everything was clean. Sterile. Ready for the next week. The cubicles were empty. The phones were silent. Sound worked differently here. It carried but stopped before it should. Like the open cubicle environment ate the noise before it could travel.

On Saturdays, only a handful of people were there. The office was a ghost town. During the week it would be packed, every desk occupied, every phone ringing. Because I was shorter than the cubicle walls, I could navigate the maze like a secret agent. Pop up in unexpected places.

My aunt went to her desk. I went to her friend's cubicle next door. The desk had the usual things. Photos of family. A coffee mug. Some kind of fidget toy thing. A massive CRT monitor taking up half the desk, generating enough heat to warm a small room.

The chair spun. I sat down. Pushed off with my feet. Started spinning. One rotation. Two. Three. Four. Five. Six. On the sixth spin, I couldn't stay in the chair anymore. My feet hit the floor. The chair kept going without me. I was aimed away from the window. Good thing too. Didn't want to see that city skyline spinning.

My aunt was on a call. I could see her through the gap in the cubicle walls. A customer needed their claim taken care of. I didn't understand business lingo back then. But I could tell something was off. The customer wasn't giving the information my aunt needed.

My aunt asked for it. Politely. Nothing. She asked again. Different way. Still polite. Nothing. Third time. She talked it through. Explained why she needed it. Made it make sense. This time, the customer gave everything.

I watched her face the whole time. The satisfaction when she got what she needed. When she could actually help. She finished being polite. Wished the client well. Hung up. She turned. Saw me watching. Smiled.

I also provided technical support services. The computer mice of the early 1990s had rubber balls that collected dust and debris. I appointed myself as the unofficial mouse maintenance specialist.

Armed with Q-tips and alcohol wipes, I would take the mice apart. Spin the bottom thing off to get the ball out. Clean the ball. Clean the rollers it spun against. The gunk was always black. I never knew what it was made of. But it slowed down computer mice.

When I put it back together, there was always so much more movement. Smooth. Fast. Like it was new again. Nobody watched me do it. I'd just find a mouse that needed cleaning and clean it.

I was also the little kid known for setting clocks on VCRs no matter where I went. I had a watch that was a TV remote. I could change channels at bars and restaurants. It was so much fun.

These Saturday mornings were the beginning.

My brother went to the convention center for baseball cards. I went for computers. My dad loved when they were both on the same day.

We'd walk through the double glass doors together. Concrete floors polished to a shine. The convention center opened up into a massive space. Vendors everywhere. Tables and booths as far as you could see. I was always excited to see what was the latest and greatest technology. The smell of old electronics. The sound of dot-matrix printers. Electronic beeps of various devices being tested.

Buddy worked one of the vendor booths. He saw me come in. Remembered me.

"Hey Tom," he'd say. He was my bud.

He always gave me discounts. He'd watch me lap the venue a few times before I bought anything. He knew I was looking. Comparing. Finding the best deals.

One day I found a cardboard box the size of a pallet. Full of off-lease desktops. The box was headed for scrap. Super cheap. At the bottom was the broken one.

I pulled it out. A Compaq desktop. The kind that was meant to go sideways so you could put the monitor on top of it. 486DX. Supposed to have 4MB of RAM.

Buddy came over. "That one doesn't work."

"How much?"

"Five dollars."

I handed him the money. "It'll be a fun project."

Buddy smiled. He knew.

I carried it out to the car. My dad was waiting. I put it in the trunk. Then I went back inside to look for more. Desktops weren't hard to carry. Even as a kid.

I saved it from a landfill.

I took it home. Opened it up. One of the memory chips wasn't seated right. I fixed it.

I powered it on. It ran Windows 3.1.

I upgraded it to Windows 95 with 26 floppy disks.

I collected hardware through my parents' basement. A few shelves of old computers.

But the best parts came randomly when my mom came home from bowling. Friday nights. She'd bowl with friends. Sometimes she'd come home with big black trash bags full of computer parts and tech. A friend who bowled with her got them from cleaning out buildings. I wouldn't see them until Saturday morning. We'd be in bed by the time mom got home.

Saturday morning. I'd wake up. Come downstairs. The bag would be sitting at the landing at the top of the stairs. I'd wait for my parents to get up. Wait for them to bring it to the living room while they drank their coffee.

Cartoons first. Woody Woodpecker. Snorks. Bobby's World. Then the bag.

I'd dump everything out on the living room floor. Cardboard boxes with anti-static bags. Foam protecting various cards. Cables of every length and type. Old floppy drives. ISA cards. These were the days where a computer was just a board with a bunch of slots. You added each piece separately. Sound card. Video card. Network card. Everything was so customized it was wild to look back on.

One time I pulled out a really long network cable. That was the real start of my home network.

Then at a yard sale, someone was selling two 10BaseT network cards. My brother and I bought them. Linked our computers together. No internet. But we could text each other and play Starcraft and Warcraft II.

Another time I pulled out a scanner. But not a regular scanner. This one you had to roll over the top of whatever you wanted to scan. Like using a rolling pin. It had its own card to read what you scanned. You'd roll it over text or a picture and it would capture it. I had no idea what it was at first. Had to figure it out. That was the fun part.

My bedroom had a loft bed with a desk underneath. Old computers from family friends. The old family computer. A giant laser printer sitting on top of the desk. When I turned on the printer, the lights in the house would dim. My parents would be on the other side of the house. The lights would flicker. "Tom's printing," my mom would say. I'd pop the service hatch of the printer to keep it from drawing so much power.

I would make reports about defragging our family computer. Five-page reports. I'd gather them up. Walk to the living room. My parents would be watching Seinfeld. I'd stand in front of the TV. Hold up the report.

"It's like you're reading a book," I'd explain. "And you put one page in your bedroom. The next in the kitchen. The next in the

living room. Another in the basement. Then back to the bedroom." I'd pause. Let that sink in. *"I'm putting the pages back in order. Making it faster and easier to use."*

My parents would nod. Maybe ask a question or two. They got it.

After that, they started asking if I'd help their friends with computer problems. My parents were in a ski club, and that's where the referrals started. I'd go to members' houses on weekends. Fix their computers. Word spread, and more people from the club kept calling.

1-8:
YOOPERLAND
(1988-1997)

My dad would finish work on Friday and we'd load up the minivan for the six hour drive north to the Upper Peninsula. The further we got from home, the more space opened up between streetlights. Eventually there weren't any streetlights at all.

My dad had particular tastes in music. Opera, bluegrass (partly because my mom didn't like it), and oldies stations that would drift in and out as we traveled. He was also devoted to AM radio. If there were clouds in the sky, we could sometimes pick up Detroit stations even hundreds of miles away.

My parents made a game out of the drive. First person to spot the Mackinac Bridge got a "beer" at dinner, or a "milk" in my case. We also had clipboards with checkboxes for things we saw. Police cars, deer, ducks, other animals. My dad had made the tracking sheets on his electric typewriter. You could feel the slight physical indent of each letter on the page. The scratch of a ballpoint pen on the clipboard while we hit a bump on I-75. Police cars were worth extra points.

One trip, we stopped in Mackinaw City at the foot of the bridge. We were walking the main tourist strip. One moment the air was a chaotic mix of diesel exhaust from the ferries and the thick, sugary scent of boiling waffle cones. The next, everything went silent. Completely silent. Like someone had pulled the plug on the whole town.

The sidewalk cleared in seconds. Shopkeepers moved with a practiced, quiet urgency, pulling people inside and locking the doors. My family was split in the scramble. My dad and brother went one direction. My mom and I were ushered into a t-shirt shop, the walls lined with neon colored Mackinac Island sweatshirts and rows of iron on decals.

Through the front glass of the t-shirt shop, we watched the street. A baby black bear, a teenager recently kicked out by its mother, walked down the center of the asphalt. It moved with a slow, rolling gait, completely unimpressed by the town.

We watched it amble past our window and turn toward the video rental store a few doors down. We heard about it afterwards. The bear knocked over entire shelves of VHS tapes. A teenager trapped behind the counter on crutches with a broken leg, unable to do anything but watch.

While the bear was browsing the movies, the town was transforming. The silence was shattered by the arrival of every law enforcement agency in the area. DNR (Department of Natural Resources). Local police. State police. The County

Sheriff. The DNR in their forest green trucks. For a kid, the parade of flashing lights was just as exciting as the bear.

When the bear finally emerged from the video store, it didn't look bothered. The officers were standing ready with their tranquilizer guns. The bear was carried out, its legs tied to a pole with a swarm of men holding him off the ground while he was limp from the tranquilizer. They didn't let him wander back into the woods. They removed him and took him elsewhere. Away from the city.

When the shopkeepers finally unlocked the doors, our family reunited on the sidewalk. We stood there in the humid afternoon air, looking toward the video store and the woods.

If Castle Rock was open, we'd stop there too. A natural limestone thing with 171 steps to the top. You could see Lake Huron and Mackinac Island from up there. At the base was a statue of Paul Bunyan and his blue ox Babe. Everyone stopped for photos.

My parents were good at keeping us busy. The game with spotting the bridge, the clipboards tracking animals and police cars. I rarely asked how much longer, but when I did, my dad would tell me to watch for the green mile marker signs.

When we crossed the Mackinac Bridge, the inner lanes were open metal grating. The tires didn't hum. They sang a high pitched metallic whine. Looking down through the grate, you could see 200 feet of open air and the turquoise Straits water moving below. It felt like the car was floating.

We'd end up at my aunt and uncle's house in Sault Ste. Marie. Right on the border with Canada. Their neighborhood had old gas lanterns in the front yards, the kind that used to be downtown and got lit by stilt walkers making evening rounds. They'd been converted to electricity but they still looked like the originals.

The house was a single level ranch on a wooded lot. Almost half an acre surrounded by trees.

We'd arrive late, often past my bedtime. When we got out of the car, if the wind was right, you could smell the wood stove before we even got to the door. In the summer, the dominant scent was pine trees. That smell was comfort.

Inside, the first thing that hit me was fresh baked cookies. It didn't matter what time we arrived. There was always a plate of them waiting, still warm.

The entry had bricks on the ground and a brick archway. After the brickwork, the floor transitioned to very comfortable carpet. So good on your feet.

Near the entry was this giant panel with like 10 light switches in a row that controlled everything for the house. I was immediately baffled by it. The kitchen had these unique switches that were little things of copper. You just had to touch them. No buttons.

The house was warm and sprawling. The wood stove sat in the center of the main living space, surrounded by comfortable seating and rocks that absorbed heat and kept radiating it long after the flames died down. When it was really going, you could hear the fire roaring.

The house was quiet otherwise. Extremely quiet compared to Metro Detroit. That silence was part of the peace.

My personal space was the two story "shed" out back. It was way more substantial than the name suggested. Upstairs was a heated guest bedroom that I almost always claimed. Cozy, with slanted ceilings and windows looking out over the trees.

Downstairs was their workshop. My uncle's side, my aunt's side. He had a pegboard covering most of one wall with what seemed like every tool ever invented. But these weren't random outlines. He had traced around each specific tool so you always knew exactly where everything belonged. A shadow board. You could see immediately if a tool was missing because the shadow was empty.

My uncle could fix anything, build anything. He'd worked all over the country before settling in northern Michigan. The tribe found him, and he spent years working in their health service.

He looked at the world completely differently than anyone else I knew. Everything was a problem that could be solved if you thought about it the right way and had the right tools.

The majority of his inventions were absolutely silent. He didn't like unnecessary noise. He'd even put a rubber band around the dog's tags to stop them from jingling.

One project that impressed me was his rainwater collection system. It wasn't a rain barrel. It was a whole network of gutters, filters, and storage tanks.

He'd also rigged up a piece of metal on a chain attached to the mailbox. When the mailbox opened, the metal would drop. You could see it from the window, so you'd know it was time to walk to the end of the driveway to check the mail. The whole thing was silent.

My aunt had her side of the workshop for pottery. She had a kiln and everything. I was always fascinated to see what projects they were both working on. My aunt gave me a small clay piece to hold my wallet. It moved with me for years.

Both of them had lived all over the country before settling in northern Michigan. Their house was filled with artifacts and souvenirs from different places. They'd bring me square coins from countries they'd visited. Aruba, I remember. The 50 cent piece. It was square. It felt wrong in a pocket full of round American quarters. It was light, aluminum and nickel, making it feel flimsy. Like play money. Spinning them felt unusual.

We'd go downtown to the Soo Locks to watch the giant freighters. These ships are massive. Over 1000 feet long. Longer than three football fields. They'd squeeze through with maybe a foot of clearance on all sides.

From the observation platform you're right there, mere feet away. You watch the water level drop in complete silence. Gravity moves the water in and out.

We'd go to the city park on the western edge of the city. Sandy beach looking out toward the shipping channel. The big boats moved surprisingly fast and quiet through the open water. The air was crisper than home and smelled of pine and fresh lake water.

After the locks we'd eat at the Lockview across the street. Second floor. You could watch the lock gates while you ate. I always got the whitefish.

1-9:
THE WILD PLACES

(1988-1997)

My uncle would often take us to local powwows. These gatherings were beautiful. Colorful, musical celebrations with traditional dances, songs, crafts, and foods. The smell of food cooking mixed with incense burning.

The dancers wore outfits with detailed beadwork, feathers, bells. Everything jingled when they moved.

The Jingle Dancers were my favorite. Their outfits were covered in little jingles. When hundreds of dancers moved together, the sound was like falling rain. My uncle said it was a healing dance. The sound was hypnotic.

In those days, crossing into Canada was easy and casual. Just a birth certificate or driver's license. A two minute interaction with a friendly guard. The Canadian side was bigger, with more options. My aunt and uncle would take us on mountain hikes in the Canadian wilderness with their dog, ending at a little restaurant that looked like it came from Europe. Totally out of place in the Ontario woods.

We went to Tahquamenon Falls a lot. The water was amber colored. Something about the cedar swamps upstream.

The upper falls drops nearly 50 feet over a 200 foot wide ledge. You can hear the roar from far away. The amber water and powerful flow. The water created a thick, brown foam at the base of the falls. The foam looked thick enough to touch, but you couldn't get close enough.

Our beagle came with us on one trip. He was usually a lazy dog, but he was always game to follow his boys. My brother and I took him down the stairs to the bottom sitting area where you could watch the falls. The stairs were steel grates. 94 steps. Our parents asked us to count to double check.

Going down, the dog was too busy keeping up with us to look down. We shot down those stairs. We'd done them so many times.

On the way back up, he realized he could see through the grates. He scrambled back up those stairs as fast as he could.

We also explored Whitefish Point, a peninsula extending into Lake Superior. There was a lighthouse that guided ships through dangerous waters. The Edmund Fitzgerald sank here during a fierce November storm in 1975.

The Great Lakes Shipwreck Museum was there. They had the bell from the Edmund Fitzgerald.

Standing at Whitefish Point, surrounded by Lake Superior going on forever, the horizon just kept going.

We'd also go to this one stretch of Lake Superior shoreline. High pines. These trees were so tall you had to crane your neck back until it hurt to see the tops. The ground wasn't dirt. It was a thick, springy carpet of brown pine needles that muffled every footstep.

The water was always shockingly cold. About 44 degrees even during the warmest summer months. But my brother and I would compete to see who could stand in the freezing water the longest.

It was pain. Actual pain. But it was also about proving I was stronger than my brother. We'd both be too stubborn to quit. We'd stand there freezing until our parents would get nervous and make us get out.

You could wade way out into the water. It was super shallow and so clear you could look for good rocks. Petoskey stones and others.

One summer trip, my mom would trade us boys for my aunt's dog for a few weeks. They'd meet halfway and do the trade. That's also where I learned to drive.

There was a Mackinac Bridge Museum tucked above a pizza shop in Mackinaw City. The tools of the ironworkers looked like medieval torture devices. Massive wrenches and rusted diving bells. Photos of men standing on the spinning cables with no harnesses.

But the real thing was the Yugo. Every Michigan kid in the 90s knew the story. 1989. A woman driving a Yugo during a windstorm. The car went over the 36 inch railing and plunged 170 feet into the Straits. The wind just picked it up. The car weighed barely 1800 pounds.

The museum had the documented history.

I just got my driver's permit and my parents did as was done to them and had me drive across the bridge. We would take turns driving and it was a total setup. The approach from the North started with a long, sweeping curve. You see the bridge in the distance, towers rising out of the water. Then you're on it.

My parents weren't saying anything. Just watching.

The inner lanes were open metal grating. The tires didn't hum. They sang a high pitched metallic whine. A vibration you felt in your chest. Looking down through the grate, you could see 200 feet of open air. The color of the water was a deep, cold Superior Blue. Even in mid-summer, the water looked like it would shatter if you dropped a rock on it.

The wind was strong that day. The steering wheel tugged toward the lake. The wind didn't just push the side of the car. It came up through the floor. Made the car feel light. Like the wind was trying to break the friction between the tires and the steel.

My palms were tacky against the wheel. Gripping tight.

The silence in the car was heavy. Everyone was waiting to see if I'd flinch or over-steer.

I didn't.

1-10:
SCHOOL DAYS
(1988-1997)

In kindergarten, someone mentioned that China was on the other side of the world. If you dug a deep enough hole, you could tunnel all the way through.

To my five-year-old brain, this wasn't a fun fact. It was a construction project.

At recess, I found a sandy area by a tree on the playground. Not many kids played there. The sand was loose, easy to dig. Perfect.

I started with a stick. Scratching at the surface, pushing sand aside. Too slow. I found a rock with a flat edge and used that instead. Better. I could scoop now, not just scratch.

The hole got deeper. I was maybe two feet down, standing in it, looking up at the playground from below. This was working.

I was so deep in the hole, literally and mentally, that I didn't hear the whistle.

Recess was over. Everyone had gone inside.

I kept digging.

Eventually I stuck my head out to get a better angle on the next section. The playground was empty.

Completely empty.

Just me and the trees and the swing sets moving slightly in the breeze.

I scrambled out of the hole. Sand in my shoes, my pockets, probably my hair. Ran to the school door and started banging on it with my little hands.

My teacher answered the door. She looked concerned.

"Tom, where were you?"

"Digging to China."

The teacher sent me to wash my hands.

That was also the year they decided I needed speech therapy.

I had a speech impediment. I couldn't talk properly.

I didn't want to admit this to you. Easier to say I was just quiet. Easier to pretend it was a choice.

But it wasn't.

They'd pull me out of class and take me to a small room with another kid or two. We'd do warm-ups. Repeat sounds. Work on letters I couldn't pronounce right.

I don't remember the specifics anymore. I've worked hard to forget them. What I remember is having to go. Having to leave class. Having to be the kid who needed fixing.

First grade was when the teacher started saying I needed new batteries.

The classroom was hot. We didn't have AC in any of the schools back then. Windows open, hoping for a breeze that most days never came. The lights were off to keep things cooler.

I'd be sitting at my desk while the teacher talked about something at the front of the room. Math, probably. Or reading. I don't remember what she was teaching.

I remember the trees outside the window.

The branches moving in whatever wind existed. The way the leaves caught the light. How they'd turn and show their undersides, that lighter green that meant the wind was picking up. Birds would land, hop around, fly off. Squirrels running along branches like they were highways.

My mind would follow them. Wonder where they were going. What they were looking for. Whether they had a routine or just moved when they felt like it.

The teacher's voice became background noise. White noise.

"Tom."

I'd blink. Look up. Everyone was staring at me.

At parent-teacher conferences, the way I remember it, the teacher told my mom I needed new batteries.

One day in third grade art class, we were making silhouette pictures for our parents.

The teacher would call us up one by one to sit in a portrait pose. She'd trace our profile on thick paper. Then we'd cut out a black piece to match it and mount it on colored paper.

The girl in front of me went up. She sat down. The teacher traced her profile.

Then the teacher said something about her shoulders. That they wouldn't be big, or something like that.

I don't remember the exact words.

The girl went back to her desk crying.

I watched this happen. My stomach dropped.

I didn't want to go up there. Whatever the teacher was saying about people's shoulders was making kids cry.

But I couldn't refuse. That wasn't how school worked.

My turn came. I walked up slowly. Sat down in the chair.

The teacher traced my silhouette. Then she looked at it and told me my shoulders would be small.

I went back to my desk trying not to cry.

I held it in. Worked on cutting out my silhouette. Mounted it on the colored paper.

My favorite part of school was choir. That started in fourth grade. Our choir teacher was passionate about music education. He actually cared that we understood what we were singing, why the harmonies worked, what the songs meant.

We did a lot of songs. One of my favorites was "Mission Control."

Mission Control, do you read me? Will you please save me a place? Mission Control, do you need me On the next rocket in space?

Maybe I'm small but I'm growing. Watch and one day you will see. Space is wide open and waiting for me.

So, Mission Control, do you read me? I really don't take too much room. Mission Control, do you need me On the next trip to the moon?

I want to study the planets. I want to study the stars. I want to go up to Venus or Mars.

I'm working hard and I'm certain An astronaut's what I will be. The sky is the limit for someone like me.

Mission Control, do you read me? I'll be seeing you in about twenty years. Until then, over and out.

My parents and my aunt were always there for my choir performances, sitting in the front rows.

But my speech therapist would frequently pull me out of choir practice for individual sessions. I couldn't understand why I had to miss something I loved and was good at.

I never told anyone about being upset about it. I held it in and went to speech therapy when they told me to.

The school computer lab was one place where things made sense.

We'd get access maybe once a month. The computers had color screens. Real color, right in my face. We played games. Money Mint taught us about making change. Number Munchers had us eating numbers while avoiding Troggles. And Oregon Trail let us ford rivers and hunt for food and watch our entire party die of dysentery.

Nobody ever made it to the end of Oregon Trail. When you died, you got to leave a tombstone for others to find on the trail. It was always fun to find other classmates' tombstones along the way.

The Snake Guy came to an assembly once with a pretty good sized boa constrictor. The snake shit all over him during the demonstration. The whole auditorium lost it laughing. The Snake Guy kept going like nothing happened.

In middle school, the typing class became a refuge. I'd eat lunch with the teacher in that classroom, away from the social chaos of the cafeteria.

A girl in my class tried for an entire month to beat me to the typing classroom every day. She didn't realize I had a secret advantage that made this competition impossible for her to win.

I ate lunch there. I was already there when she arrived breathless from running across the building.

I became obsessed with the rhythm of the electric typewriters. That satisfying strike of each key hitting the paper. The teacher would tape a sheet of paper over our hands so we couldn't look down at the keys. You had to trust your muscle memory.

That typing teacher became a real friend. Someone I trusted enough to let in on my family's favorite pizza spot, Gracie See's. Years later, she'd be my accounting teacher in high school.

In the evenings, our school offered an after-school computer club run by a math teacher who would stay late. We'd gather to connect to the primitive internet through dial-up connections. Beeps, squeaks, and electronic noise.

It was during one of these sessions that I sent my very first email. To my dad's work account.

"Hey dad this is an email from your son Tom love you."

1-11:
HIGH SCHOOL LIFE
(2001-2005)

Junior year, my marketing class period was ending when I overheard Shane, Greg, and Marc talking about the DECA meeting that night. They didn't have rides home and had to catch their bus.

I spoke up. "Hey, I can drive you guys home."

That's how it started.

They lived on the edge of the district. Far enough that I had to take the expressway one exit just to get to them. Wild to me.

The drive started on city streets. Streetlights everywhere. Then as we got further out, the houses got further apart. Eventually no more streetlights. Just open road and darkness.

The entire drive, we joked around. They had ideas for my car. Audio upgrades. Performance improvements. They were all good with cars, already working on their own.

Shane had fashion sense and an eye for camera work. When he was determined to do something, nothing would stop him. Absolutely nothing. He could read me like a book. His car had red interior lights. Under dash neon tubes. They had a distinct warm hum and took a second to flicker on. People often thought we were brothers.

Greg and I were clueless about flirting. He was a true tradesman with tools and natural abilities to do almost anything. His lights were blue. He'd figured out his car's entire audio system before he could even drive. Dual subwoofer box in the trunk. When the bass hit, the rearview mirror would vibrate so much it became useless. The kind of guy who could engineer a better way of doing anything.

Marc had purple lights. Neon strips. He knows so much about cars. How to maneuver them better. How to drive stick shift. He was really good with cars and machines and electricity. He wouldn't hesitate to take apart any part of a vehicle to fix it.

We clicked immediately.

We started making videos together. Shane and I would film everything. One day we watched an episode of COPS and figured we could make our own version. So we made it up as we went.

Months of filming on and off to make a 30 minute episode. We'd take turns being cops and robbers. Thrift store aviator sunglasses and oversized windbreakers for costumes. Heavy shoulder mounted Hi8 camcorder. Trying to hold it steady while trying not to laugh. Set up a 50mhz laptop running PowerPoint that looked like scanning a plate. An old IBM ThinkPad. Ancient even then. The thick plastic keys clacking.

Then pull someone over. All pretend and staged. Did a DUI stop with everyone in costumes for their character.

We'd discuss the outline over the week before filming. Then we'd shoot it. Take the banter pretty far until everyone in the car would just break out laughing. I don't remember specific jokes. Just that feeling of breaking character together because something was so ridiculous we couldn't keep going.

One night the real police showed up. They were driving through the neighborhood without flashing lights. Probably just doing a routine patrol check. We had all stepped inside to watch what we had just recorded. After seeing the police presence we decided to call it a night.

We made a burger commercial. A clothing company ad. Odds and ends over the years.

It was all just play.

We worked the school store together too. Sometimes you made cookies. Other times you worked the register. We'd made cookies for years. Chocolate chip, sugar, and M&M cookies. Sold them in packs of 3. Some days M&M would sell out first. Other times chocolate chip. But never sugar. Well not on my watch. Students bought ours over the cafeteria's.

Then the school administration told us there was a cease order. The cafeteria company was new, got the bid, and we violated their exclusive food service contract. Most people didn't eat cafeteria food anyway because it wasn't really good.

We found the loophole. We could sell cookies when the cafeteria was closed.

So we came to school before they opened and stayed after they closed. Dedicated. Many late nights and early mornings to make it work. Running our own black market bakery that outperformed the corporate version.

Coming in at 6:30 AM meant the hallways were empty. The school was under construction. Most hallways didn't even have ceiling tiles. Made noise and temperatures a problem. Without ceiling tiles to absorb sound, the clacking of our footsteps and the hum of the toaster oven echoed off the raw metal ductwork and the concrete waffle slabs of the ceiling. Made our black market bakery feel even more underground. Like we were operating in a half finished bunker. The smell of frozen cookie dough baking in a toaster oven. The echoing sound of your footsteps. The sound of the cash drawer. The crinkle of the small brown paper bags. Selling a 3 pack of warm cookies for $1. High volume, high satisfaction business.

DECA conferences meant longer trips. We'd convoy with the rest of the class and our teacher leading the way to the hotel. A massive 14 story glass tower. Teachers took everyone's car keys upon arrival.

The hotel hallway had that specific smell. Chlorine from the pool mixed with stale banquet food.

We'd borrow projectors from school and play PlayStation 2 in the hotel rooms. Early Epson. The cooling fan sounded like a jet engine taking off. Grand Theft Auto. Tony Hawk's Pro Skater. A 10 foot tall game projected onto the beige hotel wall. The image wasn't perfect. You'd see the texture of the wallpaper through the game. The beige stucco or vinyl pattern of the rooms gave the game a weird gridded look. A reminder we were playing a high def game in a space that wasn't built for it. Walk the mall, run into other students. Swim in the pool, hang out in the sauna, go out to dinner.

I competed as a technical marketing rep. My competition involved mock selling point of sale systems to small businesses. On premise servers. This was 2004. Cloud didn't exist yet. Pentium 4 processors and Ethernet hubs. I'd use mini CDs as part of my presentation. The 80mm pocket discs. They looked incredibly high tech and futuristic compared to standard CDs. Showing how these systems could track inventory and manage backup security. Built a whole PowerPoint around it.

The presentation was solid. Content was good. Delivery was confident.

But it was full of spelling errors. Throughout the entire thing.

I didn't ask for help. Didn't show anyone before presenting. I was afraid of being judged for not knowing better.

State conference. My parents came. Family friends came. Cousins came. All the people came.

Winners were called up on stage at the ceremony.

I wasn't called up.

I'd lost by one point. The spelling errors cost me the Visual Aids and Professionalism scores. One person proofreading would have caught every mistake.

That same conference had Data Match. The Great American Match. You took a survey on Scantron forms. Cost $3. The scanner would read your filled bubbles and a few weeks later at conference, you'd get your results. Best romantic matches. Best friend matches. Questions like Do you like long walks. Is honesty important. The analog Tinder. I actually really liked this and bought mine every year.

I got my list but was too scared to call anyone.

Then a woman called me. The hotel room phone rang. A heavy plastic chirp. I was in my hotel room. Shocked someone actually called me. I got excited.

My friends helped me clean up for it. They weren't just watching. They were huddled around the other bed whispering and stifling laughs while I tried to sound cool. One even squirted me with cologne. Axe or Curve. Chemical signal of teenage confidence.

Whatever she said made me think we'd actually connect. For once I felt like there was someone else like me.

I had no idea how any of this worked.

She asked to meet at a bench in the lobby.

I went down. Waited. The lobby was a massive atrium. Looking up from that bench I could see 14 stories of glass and steel. Made the feeling of being alone even bigger. The sound of the elevators chiming. Distant muffled music from a ballroom. Scanned every person walking past, looking for someone searching for me. Checked my watch as minutes stretched into an hour. The smell of the cologne mixing with the chlorine air of the lobby. The smell of trying too hard slowly being overtaken by the smell of a hotel lobby. The cologne fading, she wasn't coming.

Nobody came.

It hurt.

Senior year brought the Chaos Crew into my life. A mix of people who were random, playful, willing to be weird without caring what anyone thought.

On Senior Skip Day we went to a local park. Played freeze tag on the playscape. Massive wooden fort style. Built with heavy cedar 4x4s and tire swings. At 18 we weren't just playing. We could clear the monkey bars in one swing and jump from the top of the castle turret to the woodchips without thinking twice. We could climb and move faster than we did as kids. Lucky for us there were no other kids there because they were all in school. I couldn't stop smiling. That rare moment of being a kid with the physical power of a man.

Later that year they took me to Cedar Point in Ohio for a five car road trip to the amusement park.

After graduation that summer, the groups merged. DECA guys, Chaos Crew, all of us together.

One of my friends' first trips in my car, she went to roll up her window. Nothing happened when she pushed the button.

I laughed and popped the trunk. Handed her three bungee cords and a piece of plexiglass.

Before the primer went on the car looked like a cyborg. Primer grey patches with these shimmering holographic blue rings peeking through.

The boat. Land yacht. V8 engine, rear wheel drive. I'd paid $400 for it. Patched the rust holes with Bondo. Spray-painted it with primer grey I got on clearance at the hardware store.

The car never got a real color beyond that.

The chemical burn of the Bondo hardener. That pink or blue cream mixing with the grey putty. A scent that sticks in your nose for days.

Then the primer. Chalky flat texture. Didn't reflect light. Absorbed it. In the dark backroads the car was a ghost ship. Invisible until the headlights hit it.

The interior was red. Red velour. Bench seats. You could slide from driver to passenger without hitting a console. Huge back seat.

I had wired a boat light that I'd found at a garage sale into a switch on the dash. A vintage boat light. Port red and Starboard green. It was the hood ornament. I couldn't use it on public roads, but I'd use it in parking lots and when picking up friends at their homes. When combined with the red velour, the green side would look almost black and the red side made the seats look like they were glowing.

The car was unique. Lots of quirks. But that was half the fun.

We'd drive the dark back roads with no streetlights. Find the roller coaster hills where you'd crest the top and the headlights couldn't see down. Just pitch black darkness. Your stomach would drop as the car floated weightless before plunging down the other side. The heavy Mercury with soft suspension created a zero G moment. The stuff on the dashboard would actually lift off the surface for a second. CDs. Funcoland newspaper. For a split second the car wasn't steering. It was falling.

Other nights we'd pull over on the side of a dirt road next to a farmer's field on a hot humid summer night. The air would be thick and still. The field would be alive with fireflies. A silent twinkling universe. Late June and July. Thousands of them.

We'd sit there with the engine off. Listening to the ticking of the cooling metal. Watching the waves of light. A moment of pure quiet magic.

The white noise of crickets and cicadas was so loud it felt like a physical weight.

Then one night the click clack of a shotgun sliced through it like a knife.

I'd never seen everyone scramble so fast. In a land yacht the bench seat scramble is a specific move. You aren't just getting in. You are sliding across that red velour to make room for the next person. Sneakers slipping on gravel. The heavy thud of those massive doors slamming shut. The V8 didn't just start. It belched to life. Rear wheel drive meant we fishtailed on the gravel shoulder as I floored it away.

One night we went to the hills. Then the grocery store for jelly beans. Then we hiked a trail after dark, making up ghost stories along the way.

Then we drove a half hour the other way to see the legend of Reflector Man. A man who lived in a garage and played circus music. Entrance of the Gladiators. Distorted calliope music. When you turned down his street, you'd see one reflector. Then another. Then hundreds of them. The idea was that the reflectors were placed to blind you so you couldn't see the man approaching your car.

In that boat you sit so far back that the front of the car is in a different zip code. When you turn the wheel, there's a delay before the front end responds. The steering was loose. You had to anticipate every corner.

It was mainly made up. But the fear people had was wild. Especially my passenger who couldn't close their window. For them this wasn't a joke. It was a horror movie. Without the plexiglass in place the cold night air rushed in bringing the circus music sounds directly into their ear. The temperature drop. The smell of damp woods. They could hear the tall grass brushing the underside of the car. A sound that in the dark sounds exactly like someone reaching for the door handle. The hood was so long it felt like the front of the car entered the dark patch of woods five seconds before you did.

I would laugh so hard.

We'd drive until roads ended, turn around, find another one. Often we'd travel through the night, sometimes until sunrise, getting people home as the birds started chirping in the trees.

I sold that boat to my cousin for $50.

1-12:
THE G FILE
(1999-2003)

Ninth grade, second half of 1999. Computer studies class. A classroom filled with old computers that were already outdated.

The room had regular school desks in the middle for taking notes. But the real stuff was the three walls lined with Macintosh Plus computers from 1986. Already more than a decade old.

These weren't cool modern computers. They were little beige boxes that looked more like small TVs. Each one had a tiny nine inch black and white screen. Below the screen was a single floppy disk drive slot for 3.5 inch diskettes. The ones that could hold 1.44 megabytes of data.

The machines were simple. A handle molded into the top for carrying. No internal cooling fans, so they ran silent but got hot. Especially when thirty of them were running.

The school didn't have air conditioning. So we worked harder in the winter than the warmer months.

I was obsessed with the movie Hackers. Released in 1995. The aesthetic. The jargon. The gear. The acoustic coupler used on payphones. The clear cased laptop. Despite the silly 3D graphics, it captured something. The idea of exploration, social engineering, the Hacker Manifesto.

The assignments were straightforward. Simple coding exercises. Spreadsheet projects. Word processing. Many were handwritten by teachers, then photocopied. We'd get paper handouts describing what to do, then work through it.

The work came easy to me. Other students struggled with basic stuff like file management or simple programming. I just got it. I'd finish assignments way faster than the time we had. I'd finish in the first few minutes, leaving me with free time. So I started helping other students who were stuck on stuff that seemed obvious to me.

I'd watch their face while I explained something. The moment their eyes glazed over, I'd back up. Try again with smaller pieces. A classmate once stared at a loop structure for ten minutes. They were reading it bottom to top. Once I saw that, I could work with it. Find the angle that made sense to them. But first, I had to find the games.

Everyone's default password was the word GO. Password requirements didn't exist. Some friends showed off their password was changed to "password". Others used a space bar. The teacher told us passwords should be like clothing. Keep them to yourself and change them often.

I started guessing the admin password. Once per class. Didn't want to raise any alerts like in the Hackers movie. After a few weeks of trying things I could see around the school, I got it. The name of the school mascot. No special characters. No caps.

I wasn't trying to break anything. I was curious how the network worked. This was my first time seeing a computer network beyond what I had at home, where my parents' computer had two network cards and worked as the router.

My parents figured out the home network pretty quick and knew to turn off the main computer to make my brother and me go to bed. It controlled our internet.

It felt like my hacking caught up to me when I got called to the superintendent's office. But I'm getting ahead of myself.

I found what I was looking for. The master directory labeled the "G file". Stood for "Games". A treasure trove of software that was hidden behind admin restrictions.

The G file was like finding a secret arcade. It had Tic Tac Toe, an unbeatable program. MacCheckers. GNU Chess Mac. Big Al Slots, a casino slot machine game. On the Edge, a solitaire card game. Poker, five card draw. HangMan with over 2000 words that kept track of top 10 high scores.

This was around Y2K. I spent New Year's Eve 1999 in global chatrooms, talking to people all over the world. We gave each other real time updates about what happened when midnight hit in each time zone. We all thought the world might end from computer failures. It didn't. But the global communication and shared anxiety was wild.

The classroom was silent one day except for the high pitched singing of the Mac Plus power supplies. Then the

ImageWriter II at the back started its death rattle. Dot matrix printer. It had just accordion folded a sheet of continuous feed paper. The print head was trapped, buzzing against purple stained paper.

The teacher stood over it, hands on his hips, defeated.

I didn't wait. I got up, walked back, flipped the heavy plastic cover open. Released the tension on the tractor feed pins. Started backing the mangled paper out of the platen. Re aligned the butterfly holes of fresh paper onto the black plastic spikes, snapped the bar down, hit Form Feed.

The machine responded. That rhythmic, metallic zip zip zip. 1986 technology coming back to life in 1999.

I walked back to the teacher's desk. He didn't look at the printer. He looked at me. Reached down and slid open the heavy oak drawer.

In winter, the drawer had Reese's Cups. The cold Michigan air off the windows kept the chocolate firm. He'd toss one over like payment. But when the season turned and the classroom became a hotbox, heated by thirty Mac Plus motherboards with no fans, the chocolate disappeared.

In summer, the drawer had Hard Candies and Black Licorice. The only sugar that wouldn't melt in the heat.

He'd slide a piece of licorice across the desk and give me that look. "When you're in class," he'd say quietly, "I just have to watch you."

He wasn't checking if I was doing the assignment. He was just watching the only person who understood how the G file really worked and how to keep his aging lab running.

My teachers noticed I could finish work fast and help other students. They submitted my name to the district's central administration.

One day I got a note. Report to a conference room at the board of education office down the street.

I thought I was in big trouble.

I walked to the district office. The board office was in a building that felt frozen in time. Old wood paneling. Dated furniture. Institutional.

When I got to the conference room, I wasn't alone. Three other students from different schools, all looking as confused and worried as me. We sat there nervous, trying to figure out which of our questionable activities caught up to us.

The four of us talked while we waited. It was a list of potential problems and tech experiments that might have crossed the line. We'd all been pushing boundaries, exploring systems, finding creative solutions. We knew some of our stuff might not have been officially okay even if it worked.

When the superintendent came in, we braced ourselves.

"According to your teachers, you are some of the best of the best, and we would like to offer you a summer job."

Relief hit hard. Then excitement.

The superintendent explained the district wanted us to work full time over summer as tech assistants, installing hardware and setting up computer systems across all the schools for next year. We'd get paid.

It felt huge. Like what we'd been doing actually mattered enough to pay us for it.

That summer was intense. Always moving, working out of a car trunk full of disks and cables.

The district was massive. 26 buildings. Elementary schools, middle schools, high schools, a career tech center, and an alternative education building. One of the largest districts in Michigan.

We'd arrive at schools and find boxed computers and monitors. Four per classroom. One for the teacher and three for the students. Teachers would tell me computers have no place in a classroom. They disrupt learning.

My job was to unbox the desktops and monitors. Install a card in the teacher's computer to show its video on the classroom TV. We booted them to the network but it was still disk 1, disk 2, disk 3, disk 1 again. Then they'd start pulling data. Slow process.

One art teacher built paper mache around her computers. Said computers should never do art.

Setting up computers on brand new desks. We'd often spend a day in an empty school. We had to make sure the floors weren't freshly waxed, because if it hadn't cured you better not mess it up. You better check with the custodians first. Those guys were powerful beasts. But if the floors were done, it was cool to see how clean the schools were without students.

We worked full time on tech that was physically massive. Servers back then were huge. Many the size of two mini fridges back to back. Many of the servers and networking equipment needed six people to lift and move safely.

I opened one of the servers. The processor was the size of a bible. There were two of them.

There were four of us working as student tech assistants that first summer. We got close.

At the end of summer, I found out I was the only one they called back for the school year. Surprised me. I didn't realize I was different than the others. The other techs were dropped.

During the school year, I had a new title. My school's official fixer during regular hours. After school, the district's student tech specialist with access to all 26 buildings.

I got master keys to every building in the district. Two keys total. One for external doors, one for internal. Nothing was off limits.

I'd be a regular student during school hours. Well, part of it. The school asked me to fix things often when they were in a bind. So I got paged over the PA a lot. But when they weren't calling me, I was just a normal kid having a high school experience. One who had a key to the classroom. If we got to class before the teacher got back, I'd let everyone inside and we'd sit at our desks ready. Just to see them wonder if they forgot to lock the door.

My classmates found this amusing. They developed a running joke about my ability to appear anywhere in the building whenever tech help was needed.

One time I was sent a pass to come look at a computer. I told the assistant I got a test to take, I'll come by later, you can take it back. I should have just taken it. Because they called my mom at home to see where I was because they had a question and a problem to be solved. I came down after my test and we had a good laugh after they called my mom and said I'm here after all. She was just like I know he is there somewhere.

There was also the library computer lab. My senior year. We finally had the 1986 Macs replaced. The refresh hit my high school but some of the old hardware still had life in it. The computers disappeared. A woman I knew from class asked me to come with her. She's got this look on her face. "I got something special to show you." She took me to the girls bathroom on the second floor. It's all pink. She opened the door, looked around, checked it's clear and invited me in. To an outsider they'd think she was trying to seduce me into alone time. But she knew me well. She knew I would laugh really hard. And I did.

Here are piles of computers filling the bathroom. I thanked her because a bunch of us have been looking for this stash since the school year started. We figured they were trashed by mistake.

I then go to the principal and tell her I got something fun to show you, then walk her up there. We both had a good laugh. Then those computers were moved to the library for a lab down there. I started building them out. For three weeks working on them almost every free moment.

Only the day before we were going to open them to the general student population a water pipe above them broke and destroyed everything. I came in to find my coworkers and their boss there. They knew I worked hard on them. I saw the damage and said I'm going for a walk. This is during school on a closed campus. I walked to my car and drove to the nearby donut shop. Nothing a sprinkled donut can't solve. Ate my donut then came back and walked inside. The security guard said I'm sorry about your computer lab, they said they are going to get them restored, then they talked to me for a bit about never giving up, never quitting. They were wonderful. By then the bell rang and it was time to go to my social studies class and shift back into student mode.

Before I graduated, a few of the teachers made me a plaque that said "You Can't Graduate." It was a running joke, because of how much I brought to their day to day life and how much I was able to help them with things.

One of my first days after I graduated and entered my high school again, one of the assistant principals stopped me and the guy who did my role before me. He was my coworker now. He sat us down in his office, turned his laptop around and started playing a DVD. It's called "Over the Edge."

It opens with him putting a pack of cigarettes in his pocket, putting on his walkie talkie and going for a walk around the school. Finding a sandwich on the floor, picking it up and eating it. Then going around opening random lockers, grabbing them and planting the cigarettes. Then taking a student to check his locker and finding them. Then a comical montage of positions of the student taken into the office. Everything from the skeleton from the science class to him on a dolly.

They even had someone call his phone in one of the scenes. While distracted the student cuts his tie with a pair of scissors on his desk. Even wrote "stupid" on his forehead in marker. Then at the end the student pays him off with cash.

I couldn't stop laughing. That was it. I wanted to make stuff like that with my friends.

The empty schools had a strange, almost haunting vibe. Totally different from the busy, noisy environment during school hours.

A high school built for 2000 students feels like a tomb when it's just you and a server. You'd walk through a darkened hallway. The only sound being the jingle of those two master keys on your belt and the hum of the emergency lights.

Often if we were alone in the school we'd play the key game. We all had key rings of dozens of keys. The game was to see who could get closest to the last doorway of the hallway at the edge of the first of the frame. You'd toss them and slide them along the clean floors. You had to get it just right. If you got to the wall at the end of the hall you lost.

We discovered the wireless microphones in classrooms were infrared. Invisible light to communicate. You had to be in visible range of the sensor. We'd prank each other, but you could find someone because they had to be where you could see the sensor. This led to games that broke up the boring parts. We'd coordinate work, share info about problems, or just entertain each other during long installation sessions.

The following summer, I was offered full time employment again. 40 hours per week. I had money coming in.

At the end of my second summer, the administrators threw a farewell party. They told me it was time to go get a "real education." They implied I'd learned everything I could from hands on tech work and needed formal academic credentials.

Part Two:
Forging A Path

T his is the part where I built the life I was supposed to want.

Corporate jobs. A house with a mortgage. Promotions that never quite came. I was doing everything right according to the script.

I found moments of real connection here. The crew at Toys R Us, the investigators at the law firm, the friends who became family.

2-1:
THE REPUBLIC OF TOYS
(2002)

At the school district, I'd been the IT guy everyone needed but nobody wanted to deal with. Teachers would argue that computers had no place in education while I fixed their email.

At Toys R Us, everyone who walked through those doors wanted to be there.

That was the difference.

I got hired for the 2002 holiday season. Boys toys and bikes, plus register shifts mixed in. The pay wasn't great, but I didn't care. I was excited. It felt like play.

The store during early November, before the real chaos hit, had this energy I'd never experienced in a job. People would wander the aisles like they were exploring. Boxes had open fronts where you could push a button to make a car's lights flash or squeeze a doll to hear it talk. There were demo toys for everything. Kids testing stuff out, parents watching them light up.

It reminded me of being a kid at Toys R Us. The expensive video games and remote control cars were locked in giant glass cases. You'd stare through the glass, make your choice, pull a small rectangular paper ticket from a plastic sleeve on the display. You'd take that ticket to the cashier, and after you paid, an announcement would come over the PA system. "Pick up at the service booth." That walk to the service booth was the best part of the whole trip.

I was on the other side, helping create that same feeling for other kids. I was the gatekeeper behind that window, sliding out the Nintendo GameCube or PlayStation 2 boxes.

By mid-November, everything changed.

The store got hot. Not warm. Hot. All those bodies packed into the aisles. Parents, kids, grandparents, everyone hunting for the perfect gift. The heat would build through the day until you felt like you were moving through something thick.

The noise was constant. Beeping from registers. Cash drawers slamming open. Heavy metallic clack-ding. If you were on register for eight hours, that sound became a rhythmic industrial beat that followed you home. Kids yelling with excitement or frustration or both. That high-pitched shriek that only little kids can produce. The one that cuts through everything else and makes every adult in a fifty-foot radius turn their head.

And the music.

Christmas music on a constant loop. Not a radio. A curated corporate loop. By December 10th, you could predict the exact second the next song would start. You'd hear the first notes of All I Want for Christmas Is You and feel your eye twitch. The combination of music and customers talking and kids yelling got overstimulating sometimes, but I pushed through.

I knew it was seasonal. I only had to make it a few months.

That helped big time. Knowing I had an out.

The hours during the holiday season stretched until midnight. My coworkers in the video game section were a crew of stoners and adult kids who'd never quite grown out of their passion for gaming. They'd challenge each other to Mario Kart and Dr. Mario tournaments during breaks. Serious competitions. Real rivalries. Trash talk. The kind of focus you'd expect from actual athletes.

Eli handled all the bike assembly. The guy could get serious air on the BMX ramps we'd construct after hours. He could jump higher and with more style than anyone I'd ever seen.

One time I set up the ramp before he got there. Figured I'd try to get some air myself.

The ramp flew out from under me. I landed hard.

Eli showed up and laughed.

I worked boys toys and bikes mostly, but when I wasn't helping kids find action figures or stocking shelves, I was up front on the registers. That's where I saw everything.

Priests buying armfuls of toys for charity drives. Parents dropping thousands of dollars in a single transaction. Grandparents who'd saved for months to spoil their grandchildren. College students carefully counting out exact change to buy a single present.

One day I was getting a remote control car from top stock. One of them fell. A customer caught it, laughed, said his time playing sports finally paid off.

I became the sticker guy without planning it.

Geoffrey stickers from our promotional materials. Holographic circles featuring the giraffe. I'd keep a stack in my apron pocket. Ready.

One afternoon I heard it. That sound that makes every adult within range freeze.

A little girl screaming at the top of her lungs.

Not crying. Screaming. That high note that only little girls can hit. The one that gets everyone's attention whether they want it or not.

I didn't know why she was screaming. Didn't matter why. All that mattered was making it stop.

I grabbed a Geoffrey sticker and moved fast. Crouched down to her level, made eye contact, held out the sticker like it was treasure.

"Hey, do you want to meet Geoffrey?"

The screaming paused mid-shriek. Tiny fingers reached for the giraffe sticker. The mother mouthed "thank you" while the crisis dissolved into fascination with shiny paper.

I also kept a small stash of the hottest, most in-demand toys hidden in the back room. Products that were officially sold out but that I could access for special circumstances.

The most memorable one involved a dad who'd been searching for specific Beyblades his son desperately wanted for Christmas. Metal-fusion spinning tops. The Dragoon and Dranzer models. Small, hard to find. He'd driven to every Toys R Us in a three-hour radius. Spent entire weekends visiting different stores, calling ahead to check inventory.

When he first approached my register, he was rude. Yelling at me about our lack of stock, treating me like I was personally responsible for global supply chain issues. His frustration made sense, but his approach wasn't helping.

Instead of matching his hostility, I looked at him directly. "Excuse me, are you okay?"

He broke down right there in the checkout line. Crying in front of other customers about his fears that he was failing as a father. Worry about not being able to provide the kind of Christmas his son was hoping for.

The shift happened fast. One second yelling, next second breaking down.

I don't know where the words came from. "It doesn't matter what gift you bring them. It's about the time you spend with them and showing them that they matter to you. The specific toy isn't what they'll remember twenty years from now."

Then I added, "And I happen to have a Beyblade in my personal stash that I've been saving for exactly this kind of situation."

I went to the back room and retrieved it. Whether he absorbed the message about quality time, I'll never know. But in that moment, it felt right.

The employee breakroom became my sanctuary.

It was painted that same Toys R Us blue that covered the whole store. One wall had a bulletin board plastered with notices. Required by law postings. Shift schedules. Notes of gratitude from kids. Thank you drawings in crayon.

There was a table. Chairs. A TV mounted in the corner showing a camera feed of the front of the store. Grainy 13-inch monitor.

I'd make myself a peanut butter and honey sandwich. JIF on white bread. The honey would soak into the bread, creating a sealed sweetness that didn't get soggy. Energy dense. Quick energy, lasting satisfaction, didn't require much time or money.

Then I'd sit at that table and watch the TV. The camera showed the front doors, the registers, all the chaos I'd just walked away from. I could see it happening right there on the screen.

Like it wasn't happening right outside the door.

The madness was contained in that little TV. I was watching from a safe distance. I could watch it without being in it. The noise was muffled. The heat was on the other side of the wall. For fifteen minutes, the screaming kids and the Mariah Carey loop were just images on a screen, unable to touch me. For fifteen minutes, I could breathe.

One day I got sick. Really sick. Still had to work. I was on register when my stomach started turning. I started gagging. Told the customer "I'll be right back," turned off my light, ran to the restroom, came back and finished the transaction.

The worst day was when a Code Adam got called. A missing kid. The store went into lockdown mode. Everyone dropped everything, went to stations, started searching. I wasn't boys toys guy anymore. I was security. Every employee moved to a designated door. We found him pretty quickly. Turned out he was a teenager, not a little kid. But those few minutes before we found him, my heart was pounding.

The work was physically demanding in ways I hadn't anticipated. Each shift was a blur of long hours. By the end of each day, the store looked like a hurricane had hit it. Aisles that had been perfectly organized in the morning were now disaster zones. Opened boxes. Try Me buttons dying. Toys from the back of the store left in the front.

But we were a tight crew. We'd stay late after the store closed, working together to restock shelves, reorganize displays, prepare for the next day. Once the doors locked, we took over. The stoners from the R Zone, Eli the bike-jumper, and me. We'd work in a flow state, restocking shelves and zoning the products until the aisles were perfect ninety-degree angles again. Putting everything back together. Our laughter would echo through the empty aisles as we shared stories and made jokes. We'd convert the ransacked disaster of closing time into the pristine wonderland that customers would encounter when we opened the next morning.

At the end of a twelve-hour shift, I was exhausted. Ready to sleep and do it again.

2-2:
THE BINDER CLIP
(2003-2004)

My first corporate job wasn't in some sleek office building. It was inside a massive manufacturing plant that produced advertisements for newspapers. The marketing company had set up headquarters alongside the production equipment.

The air inside smelled like ink. Always ink. Heavy, oily, metallic newspaper ink mixed with industrial solvents. The air was so thick you could almost taste it.

On days they were running specialized print, the smell got worse. The specific ink used for scratch-off applications released a different kind of odor. Burnt plastic and rotting sulfur. A chemical stench that stuck to your clothes. So stinky that I actively avoided the plant part of the building when they were running that stuff.

My official title was IT Support Intern, but my actual work went throughout the entire complex. Air-conditioned office areas where account executives worked on campaigns. Production floor where massive printing presses operated around the clock. I had to support both worlds. Office workers who needed help with email. Production floor emergencies when a press went down during a big run.

Moving between the office and the plant meant passing through the high-speed roll-up doors. Giant vinyl curtains that moved at eighty inches per second. I'd hit the button and hear a powerful zing-whoosh as the curtain vanished into the ceiling. The air pressure would change instantly. Cool, filtered office air being sucked out into the humid, ink-heavy heat of the plant. I kept to the unwritten industrial rule. Leave it as you found it. If the door was down, I waited for it to reset.

The manufacturing floor had its own culture. Its own humor. Its own way of testing newcomers. Their favorite target was the IT intern. Me. Their preferred method was elaborate wild goose chases.

One successful prank involved convincing me there was a "glue warehouse" in the paper warehouse basement. They gave me detailed directions, complete with warnings about confusing corridors and the importance of bringing specific tools.

The warehouse floor was clearly demarcated by yellow lines. I followed these lines like they were a map, walking past those giant vinyl doors. Kept to that same rule. Leave the door in the state you found it.

I spent the better part of an afternoon following the lines to the back corner, searching for a nonexistent stairwell.

The warehouse was a single-story corner with a concrete slab foundation. No basement anywhere.

When I figured it out, I'd found a good spot during my wandering. That back corner where the yellow lines ended. That wasn't a stairwell entrance. It was a legally mandated fire break. A specific marking on the ground preventing the massive paper stacks from touching the wall.

The giant rolls of paper absorbed every noise. Each roll weighed nearly a ton. So dense and fibrous they acted as perfect acoustic absorbers. Stepping into that back corner by the yellow fire-break line was like stepping into a soundproof room. The roar of the presses and the constant beeping of forklifts didn't just get quieter. They were erased. In that dead silence, I could finally hear my own breathing. Safe mode for my brain.

When I returned to the guys who'd sent me on this mission, I thanked them for helping me find such a great hiding spot.

Treating their prank as a favor.

Another memorable initiation involved an electrician who worked on the complex electrical systems. They handled the high-voltage 480V three-phase power that ran the presses. I was in an electrical room carefully resetting a circuit breaker when he snuck up behind me and scared me so badly that I could have sworn I briefly achieved flight.

The adrenaline zing in my fingertips. My heart trying to exit through my ribs. The startle was so intense that for a moment I was convinced I'd touched the ceiling. But I laughed it off.

Then came the crisis that changed everything.

The problem involved a critical database server attached to a massive storage system. Twenty hard drives working together, the whole thing the size of a mini-refrigerator. It managed all the production schedules, inventory tracking, and complex coordination required to ensure the right advertisements got printed for the right newspapers on the right dates.

When it started showing signs of failure, everyone in management began to panic.

The beeping of the controller. Not a soft chirp. A piercing alarm designed to be heard over the roar of printing presses. Constant. Insistent.

Red lights flashing when it was in distress.

Performance slowing down. Warning messages about drives failing. This thing going down meant production stopped, deadlines missed, serious revenue lost.

While senior staff huddled together making phone calls to vendors and researching replacement options, I was alone with the failing system, studying it.

I wasn't panicking. It was easily fixable. I had to find the problem.

I opened up that server. The heat hit my face like an oven. Waves of heat coming off those spinning drives.

The problem wasn't the hard drives themselves. One of the array's cooling fans wasn't functioning properly, causing the entire system to overheat and become unstable. The fan was there, it was plugged in, but it wasn't making proper contact to spin. The connection was soldered to the board, but the solder point was weak. A tiny crack where the metal didn't bond right. A light touch of my finger could make the fan work again.

The solution was a single binder clip.

A medium 1.25-inch black clip with silver wings. I popped the controller drawer out just enough to fit the binder clip on the edge. The clip acted as a simple pressure device, ensuring the connection held. I positioned it so the black spring-steel body clamped the connector firmly against the board, then I snapped the silver wings off. It stuck out and looked weird, but it worked.

Within thirty minutes, and for the cost of five cents of office supplies from the supply closet, the entire RAID array stabilized and returned to normal operation.

The beeping stopped instantly. The red lights turned green.

Everyone had been running around in crisis mode. I fixed it with a binder clip.

I was excited. That simple fix earned me credibility. More than that, it felt good. The presses kept running. The deadlines were met. And I'd done it with office supplies.

I got to observe the whole creative process. Account executives managing clients. Creative directors developing campaigns. I could see how their worlds all connected.

One memorable project for the end-of-summer intern program was a short video our team created called "Coming to Work."

We filmed it on a digital camcorder in the parking lot one morning.

First shot: One guy cruises in slowly, early, smooth. Gets the prime parking spot right up front.

Second shot: Me. Sprinting across the parking lot. Tie flying. Barely making it.

Third shot: The last guy. Rolling in late. He sees the expectant mother parking spot. Looks around. Steals it.

We'd gotten her permission and moved her car for the shot. She thought it was hilarious. We coordinated it valet-style, everyone playing their parts.

The whole thing captured our company culture perfectly. It wasn't complex. Just a simple joke that landed.

After the binder clip fix, the electricians presented me with a pocket protector. At first, I thought it was a joke, some kind of nerd hazing. But then I noticed the color. Red.

Turns out, that meant something. If you had a red pocket protector, it meant the electricians had your back. And if they had your back, nobody on that floor would mess with you. It was a status symbol I hadn't known existed.

I felt honored wearing it.

Brett was one of the guys from the office side. We'd go on cross-country trips together to upgrade computers. He was on my first flight. He had advice on everything. Those trips were my introduction to corporate IT at scale.

Then came the Great Blackout of 2003.

There was a woman on the office side I thought was really cool. She called me about an issue with her computer. I got excited and went over there. Nervous.

I crawled under her desk and checked the port. The lights on the network jack weren't lighting up all the channels correctly. I told her we'd have to go to the back room where all the ports terminated to re-punch it down. I asked if she wanted to come with me. She said yes, she was curious to see.

So we went back there. I was a little nervous. I re-punched the port down, verified with the tester that it looked good. Then I turned around and tripped. Fell. Tore a couple cables out of the patch panel.

At that exact moment, the lights went out.

Then I heard all the machines in the plant, the constant hum you'd hear from the hallway, come to a stop. Everything went silent and dark. The little emergency lights clicked on.

I walked her back to her desk and headed for the building's data center. At the time, we only had batteries. Maybe half an hour to an hour before systems would be forcefully shut down. A couple coworkers met me there, and we started picking and choosing which critical systems needed to be properly shut down first. Moving as fast as we could. It was a race against time.

That's when we started getting word. The power wasn't just out here. It was out across the entire eastern seaboard.

The worst shifts were the 3am server migrations. You'd be in the empty building, completely alone except for the hum of the servers. After being awake that long, everything got loopy. You'd start seeing things that weren't there. Hear footsteps in empty hallways. The fluorescent lights would buzz and you'd swear they were getting louder.

We'd migrate data from old systems to new ones. Hours of watching progress bars. Making sure nothing corrupted. One wrong move and you could lose everything.

The best times were the late nights. After about 9pm, there'd be nobody else in the building but us. People doing system upgrades, working on projects that couldn't happen during business hours. We'd grab chocolates from the candy dishes people left on their desks for the office. The blue light of the computer monitors reflecting off the crinkled wrappers in a dark office at midnight. The company paid for our dinners when we worked late, then we'd stay up super late and come back before anyone else arrived in the morning.

We'd pull pranks on each other. Talk about anything and everything. Those nights had an energy to them. A sense of being part of something. Working on systems that kept the whole operation running, doing it when nobody else was around to see it.

The culmination was being selected to receive the "Intern of the Year" award. The ceremony was held in the company's main auditorium.

But in a perfect twist, the audiovisual system chose that exact moment to malfunction. Of course, I was called to the front to diagnose and repair the problem in front of the entire company while wearing my best professional clothes. Starch-collared shirt and khakis.

I crawled under the table to fix the AV system. Found a video cable that had been intentionally loosened just a hair. I tightened it. The screen flickered to life. Gave the thumbs-up to the AV booth.

The sudden roar of applause.

The moment I sat down, they called my name.

The "technical problem" was the prank. They'd gotten me perfectly. The whole company was in on it.

But the real surprise came when I looked into the audience and saw my parents sitting in the crowd. They were beaming with pride, documenting the moment with their cameras. Someone had told them about the ceremony. They'd shown up without telling me.

The award was a plaque. Intern of the Year. My name engraved on it.

Glory.

After the ceremony, they offered me a full-time employee position.

I accepted.

The award plaque sat on my desk for years. The binder clip? I kept that too, in my toolkit.

2-3:
THE STYLISH MUSTACHE
GOES TO JERSEY
(2006)

The idea was born at Jon's Goodtime Bar & Grill during trivia night.

Jon's was the kind of place that never changed. You'd step off the bright, busy street into a dim, wood-paneled tunnel. It was a shotgun-style building, long and narrow, with booths in the middle each forming their own little cubby, a bar running along one side, our table in the back corner, and my parents' table in the front middle. The kind of comfortable neighborhood tavern where everyone was included, where my mom often made cupcakes for everyone's birthday, including strangers and barflies, and where you could get reliable burgers and famous fish and chips without breaking the bank.

We were regulars at trivia night. Our team, "The Stylish Mustache," often found ourselves pitted against my parents' team, "The Dream Team." We were good on pop culture and anything from the 90s forward, and we'd recruited a friend's aunt for history and other areas where we were weak. My parents' team was really good. Seasoned veterans who could nail 70s rock questions and world capitals with surgical precision.

The playful banter back and forth between our tables was some of the best fun I'd had. We weren't just playing trivia. We were performing for the regulars. My parents' table in the front middle, our table in the back corner, and everything in between became the stage. At halftime, everyone would pile into the middle of the bar for a two-song dance break before sitting back down for the second half. I was drinking martinis, trying to channel James Bond, while most people stuck to beer.

We had a strict designated driver policy for our group. One person stayed sober and drove everyone home, then the next morning we'd all get dropped off at our cars.

Shane started scrolling eBay on his Palm Treo 650, what was still a novelty, one of the first smartphones. The tiny backlit screen glowed as he showed us listings for increasingly ridiculous items people were selling online. Vintage arcade games, military surplus, someone's collection of ceramic unicorns. Each click of the center navigation button was another gamble, the full QWERTY keyboard click-click-clicking as he refreshed the bid page.

Then he found the bus.

It was a short bus from 1994 that was twelve years old, sitting in a dirt lot somewhere in New Jersey. Shane's pitch was simple. We should buy it for mountain biking adventures. He was a rum and pineapple kind of guy, and none of us wanted to listen to reason. We wanted a bus.

"We should buy it," Shane announced, with the kind of casual certainty that only emerges after several drinks and the adrenaline rush of correctly identifying the capital of North Dakota.

Amy immediately started listing reasons this was a terrible idea. The distance. The mechanical unknowns. The insurance. The storage. But she was laughing while she said it, the same way she laughed at all our ridiculous plans. "Shane. It's a twelve-year-old bus. In Jersey."

Shane didn't even look up from the Treo. "You're not my wife."

The table erupted.

The next morning, Shane texted me. He'd won the auction. He owned a school bus.

I was excited. It was a childhood dream to have a school bus. It's wild how fast a drunk idea becomes a real road trip.

We started planning the adventure. Leave after work Thursday, drive through the night, get there Friday morning, grab the bus, drive back, be home by Friday night. Most people didn't bring extra clothes. Nobody planned for hotels. The plan was nothing like what happened.

The first MapQuest printout came out at exactly 666 miles. Three or four stapled pages with turn-by-turn directions. When we saw that number, someone pulled out a paper Rand McNally atlas and manually found a different route just to break the curse. One rental car, five people, and enough caffeine to keep us alert for the round trip.

We made it about halfway before the fog rolled in.

The mountains of Pennsylvania disappeared into a gray soup so thick you could barely see the taillights of the car ahead of you. White knuckle silence filled the rental car. The only sounds were the hum of the heater and the rhythmic thump-thump of the tires on the Pennsylvania Turnpike expansion joints. Sleep deprivation and near-zero visibility forced us down to 55 mph on highways where we should have been doing 70. After hours of driving inside a cloud, we admitted defeat and pulled into a Holiday Inn Express.

Six hours of sleep and a continental breakfast that we treated like an all-you-can-eat buffet to make up for the unexpected expense. The lobby air smelled like waffles from the waffle iron. We were the loudest group in the place, fueled by sleep deprivation and excitement. We loaded our pockets with muffins and fruit, approached the waffle station like we were stockpiling for winter, and generally behaved like people who understood the economics of roadside hospitality.

We arrived in New Jersey around 2:30 PM to find the bus yard nearly empty. All the buses were off doing their jobs, transporting kids to and from school. But there, in the corner of the lot next to a huge puddle, was our new baby.

The sellers asked where our trailer was. We laughed and said we were driving it back. They were most amused by this revelation and immediately started fixing little things to make the journey smoother. Adding a mirror, replacing seat bottoms, installing light covers. They told us we had "big balls" for even attempting the drive and seemed genuinely invested in giving us the best chance of making it home alive.

The moment the engine turned over, I knew we were in trouble. Something about the sound it made, the way it shuddered before settling into an idle that was more suggestion than certainty. "Kids must have died in this thing," Shane muttered, only half-joking.

As if the universe wanted to confirm my suspicions, the radio crackled to life the moment we started moving, Tom Petty's "Breakdown" filling the cabin. We turned it off immediately.

The first major crisis hit after we crossed into Pennsylvania. The bus started spewing a strange smoke screen that coated the rental car following behind, creating a visibility problem that quickly attracted attention.

First came the PennDOT support trucks. Three bright orange work trucks with massive yellow flashing arrow boards on the back. They didn't just pull over. They blocked the lane, the yellow lights pulsing. You could hear the high-pitched chirp as they backed up, and the heavy diesel rattle even inside the bus.

Then the Pennsylvania State Trooper arrived. White car with blue and gold stripes. He stayed in the car for a moment, lights flashing.

When he stepped out, he looked incredibly professional. The whole uniform was grey and black, polished to perfection.

While waiting for the tow truck, out of sheer boredom, a few of us decided to climb the tall, grassy embankment on the side of the road. A massive semi-truck sized tow truck arrived. The driver took one look at us scattered across the hillside and started yelling warnings about ticks.

Too late.

Everyone started frantically checking themselves. Ticks were everywhere. On the seats. On the floor. Crawling up pant legs. The bus turned into complete chaos. People jumping up, smacking at their clothes, yanking off shoes. Someone was banging on the bus door trying to get it open wider. Everyone itching phantom sensations, convinced every tickle was another tick. The tow truck guy had a good laugh over this one. He was wonderful.

The tow truck driver said it would be cheaper if they didn't hook up the bus and had us follow him to a shop in the middle of nowhere. We dropped off the bus and discovered the shop wouldn't be open until Monday, three days away, since it was a holiday weekend.

As soon as the tow truck driver left, we realized the bus drove fine. We'd learned that slower speeds worked way better.

We were faced with a decision. Drive it home or leave it at the repair shop?

We decided to drive home.

First stop was the nearest 24-hour Walmart. We grabbed fire extinguishers and walkie-talkies. Just in case things got sticky.

We drove for four or five hours without any problems. Finally decided it was time to get some rest. Another hotel.

That's when Emily found the tick attached to her in the shower, letting out that blood-curdling scream that haunted us all.

We became a traveling tick inspection unit, constantly checking each other for signs of unwanted passengers.

The next morning, feeling defeated and wearing the same clothes for days, we stopped at Cracker Barrel for breakfast. After breakfast, several friends made a run through the gift shop, emerging in identical Heather Green t-shirts with a yellow and black tractor on the chest. Brand new, unwashed, with that factory smell and sharp fold lines still crisp across the chest. Overpriced tourist merchandise that at least made us feel human again. We sat looking out the window at the bus, five exhausted, tick-paranoid people in matching stiff gift-shop shirts. Nobody commented on the matching shirts.

He walked us back to the bus. Looking at the paint and dirt on the bus you could tell it hadn't moved in years. "You kids have some serious balls," he said, wiping his hands on a rag. "Driving a twelve-year-old bus from Jersey."

Back on the road, we started going silent, switching drivers between the hot bus and the rental car with AC. It was 88 degrees. If only that 88 were in miles per hour, we could go back to the future and buy a bus from a nearby rich local school district instead.

As if on cue, the radio started playing AC/DC's "Highway to Hell," which we quickly turned off.

It was late afternoon. The sun was getting lower. That golden hour light.

Our walkie-talkie crackled to life. It was the rental car. "You need to pull over now. The smoke has gotten dark. We may have a problem."

We pulled over immediately on the shoulder.

Shane popped the main hood. Nothing visible. Everything looked fine.

Then I opened the inner doghouse cover on the other side of the engine.

Flames.

Actual flames licking up from the engine compartment.

"FIRE!" I yelled.

Everyone scrambled. One person grabbed the fire extinguisher we'd bought at Walmart. Started spraying. White chemical fog filled the engine bay.

The rest of us bailed out the back emergency door.

I stood there on the shoulder watching. Laughed. Of course the bus was on fire. Why wouldn't it be?

In what felt like seconds, semi drivers were pulling over. Strangers were running from their cars with their own fire extinguishers.

People were helping us. Complete strangers stopping on a highway to put out our bus fire.

The flames died down. The extinguisher powder covered everything. The engine compartment looked like someone had dumped a snowstorm inside it.

I laughed. It was one thing after another.

Then we saw it. A silver State Trooper car backing up on the shoulder toward us. The Ohio State Trooper.

He took one look at our adrenaline-filled bodies and our increasingly battered bus and shook his head. "You guys have some serious balls for driving an old vehicle like this," he said. "Looks like it sat for years."

Yeah, we were starting to figure that out.

We sat there on the shoulder, everyone's adrenaline dumping hard. A few minutes later, the trooper came back and asked if we thought we could nurse it off the highway to a service plaza just ahead.

When we tried to move it, there were no problems. As long as we kept it at 55 mph or less, it drove fine.

At the service plaza, the group's morale finally broke. A vote was held to abandon the bus. The motion passed 3-2.

Shane and I were stubborn. We kept going.

Everyone else hugged us goodbye and piled into the rental car. It was just Shane and me in the bus.

We drove the rest of the way in silence. Constant radio checks with the rental car following behind. Keeping speeds low. Watching everything. Every time we stopped, we checked for fire.

Our first stop back in town was to drop off the overdue rental. The company was starting to complain about how late we were, but one look at our exhausted, grimy crew and they mercifully let it go.

With the rental car gone, we had no choice but to pile everyone into the bus for the very last leg of the journey. The final twenty minutes were especially tense. The transmission kept popping out of gear, and nursing the bus through residential streets felt like walking a mechanical tightrope.

We finally pulled into the driveway as it was getting dark. The backup beeper screamed our arrival to the entire neighborhood, the loudest, most obnoxious sound in a quiet street. It was the Stylish Mustache announcing that the mission was accomplished, even if the bus was currently held together by luck and Cracker Barrel muffins. Shane walked into his house to discover a surprise birthday party that our friends had organized while we were gone, complete with bus-themed decorations.

But that was the beginning.

The bus became our project for the next several months. Shane's dad, the guys in the group, including me, did most of the work, spending weekends and evenings replacing the old seats with conversion van seats. We left the old seats in until the new ones arrived we'd found on Craigslist. We'd show up to pick up parts with a bus full of people, opening the folding door to reveal an entire board of directors sitting on the floor of a gutted bus just to buy one bench seat. The sellers always looked confused.

Our workdays always started with a meeting inside the gutted bus, all of us sitting on the floor. The acoustic echo inside that hollow metal shell made every word bounce off the windows. For fifteen minutes, we'd have an open discussion, creating a plan of attack and figuring out what made the most sense before we even picked up a tool. It was the war room where we moved from being guys with a bus to engineers with a mission.

Then we got to play. We fired up angle grinders, sanders, and sawzalls, learning as we went. We were smart about it, always wearing masks and safety glasses because flying metal shavings are no joke. Sparks flew, but we were careful, making sure to wear clothes that wouldn't light up in an instant.

Our biggest challenge was the non-working wheelchair lift. After we tore it out, the four of us couldn't even budge it. We biked, so we had legs, but not the kind of arms needed for that dead weight. It lay in the yard until two massive scrappers came by one day. They picked the thing up like it was nothing, carried it to their truck, and threw it in the back. We were as thankful as they were. We gave them all the old metal seats and parts we'd gutted. They got a good haul, and we got our problem solved.

We installed a removable sofa.

Then came the painting party. Blue and orange with a stripe, all done with rollers. Lots of people showed up, and by the end of the day, the bus looked fantastic.

We were the Helmet Heads, a mountain bike team. We'd had that name for a while, so we painted it on the side of the bus. A few months later, some stranger stopped us and asked if we had any idea that could be offensive. We added "mountain bike team" underneath.

Once it was road-ready, it became our group adventure vehicle. We'd designate one person to stay sober and drive the rest of us wherever chaos called. One day we took on a 1-pound burger challenge. None of us succeeded. It was painful and hilarious, and the bar staff was amazed we'd shown up in our own bus.

Another time we went to a drive-through animal safari and broke down as soon as we got past the last safety gate. The alternator gave out. Staff in golf carts surrounded the bus to keep animals away while we waited for the tow truck. The friends who went with the tow truck said the Jesus bobblehead on the dash bobbled the entire ride, nodding approval to every bump in the road, all the way to a yard filled with buses, ambulances, and vans. They had the parts, fixed it cheaply, and met the rest of us at a local bar. We never did see the safari.

That day we'd parked in an alley because the bus didn't fit in most parking spots. Delivery trucks blocked us in, so we sat around telling stories from the group's past, all the chaos we'd created over the years. I kept messing with whoever was in the driver's seat by pulling the fire alarm on and off. It wasn't a beep. It was a vibrating metal diaphragm, a teeth-rat-tling BZZZZZZZT designed to be heard over a roaring diesel engine and 30 screaming kids. The whole dashboard hummed. Then it got stuck.

I laughed, ran to the front, said I needed to remove a panel to disconnect the power. Behind it was a rat's nest of wires, brittle 12-year-old insulation that had been baked by the New Jersey sun. I wasn't just touching a wire. I was touching the bus's central nervous system. I read the schematic wrong. It wasn't a tingle. It was a high-amperage kick that felt like a punch to the chest, a metallic taste flooding my mouth. I hit the floor and my fight-or-flight kicked in. I ran just outside the bus before my firefighter friend caught up to me. He had a 6th sense for this kind of thing. He did an assessment, checking my pulse while I could still taste copper, and advised I see a doctor, but I refused over and over. Instead, we went for milkshakes.

The bus went to parades and weddings. We used it for mountain biking trips constantly. I built a mountain bike rack out of PVC. A spine made of 2-inch pipe that ran along the floor, with stanchions that cradled the front tires. I used heavy-duty bungee cords to tension the frames against the bus's ribs so they wouldn't sway when we hit Michigan potholes. The scent of purple PVC primer and the thick, sweet-chemical smell of the cement lingered for a week. We could open the rear wheelchair door to load bikes in and out.

When I worked at the law firm, I'd pick up coworkers who were in town for a case and give them tours of Detroit. I'd be up front, maneuvering that massive thin-rimmed steering wheel, while they sat on the Craigslist conversion seats. The ultimate pattern interrupt. They'd expect a town car and get a blue-and-orange short bus with a PVC bike rack in the back. That's where I got the nickname Tour Guide Tom. I wasn't just driving. I was connecting the nodes of Detroit, pointing out the hidden engineering of the city.

We used that bus for two or three years, fixing problems as we found them, creating memories at every breakdown and triumph. When life circumstances changed and I knew I was losing the house in a sheriff sale, Shane sold it on eBay to a dance studio down south.

2-4:
SCARS AND GUARDIAN ANGELS
(2006)

It started as one of those perfect, unexpected gifts. A half day off work on a 70 degree day without a cloud in the sky. Warm air, birds chirping, nice breeze. The kind of day that demanded an adventure, so I started calling friends for a last minute mountain bike ride.

Crazy how fast the best days can flip.

The ones who were free were my younger buddies. A fearless crew of BMX riders. They were always on bikes. One was twenty-one, three were twelve to fifteen years old. I went around and picked everyone up in my car. We headed for a state park, a trail I knew well but that was constantly evolving. The local riding community was always adding new, more difficult features. Jumps, balance beams, log piles, turning familiar woods into a place of constant new challenges.

At the trailhead, we screwed up. Five guys, five bikes, but only four helmets. Didn't seem like a big deal. I offered mine to Marc, my twenty-one-year-old buddy who was new to this trail, but he said no. "I'll go slow," he promised, "and stay in the back." He'd been there for me for years as one of the DECA guys. We made sure the first-timers all had helmets. Since we had people new to the trail, we split gear between the bikes. First aid kit, extra water, tools.

I took the lead, yelling back basics of shifting and tricks to the trail. I could feel their energy behind me, pushing me to go faster. I really got going, far enough ahead I couldn't tell who was behind me.

I hopped a log and got to the crossing for one of the service roads. A steep, paved hill. I rode to the top and started bombing back down, picking up serious speed. None of us knows what went wrong. My best guess is the new bike. My old bike had disc brakes where the harder you squeezed, the harder it stopped. This new bike had V-brakes. Rubber pads that grabbed the metal rim directly. On that steep hill, I was carrying serious speed. When I squeezed those brakes, they didn't slow me down smooth. They locked. The pads grabbed the rim so hard the front wheel just stopped. The bike stopped dead, but I kept going. Launched me over the bars.

Nick, riding behind me, saw me flying through the air and, for a split second, thought I was messing around, showing off. Then he saw me land, hard, on my shoulder and face. I road rashed myself right through my shirt and was out cold.

The next thing I knew, I was dreaming and sweating. My face was soaked. I started to wonder how I didn't remember the rest of the bike ride or evening.

But even unconscious, I had priorities. According to my friends, when I first came to, I kept ranting about finishing the trail. Over and over. "I have to finish the trail. We can't leave. I have to finish the trail." They said it took several minutes to convince me that finishing the ride wasn't the most important thing right then. They had to hold me down.

As my friends pulled up one after another, a new kind of panic set in. Nobody had a cell phone. This was still the era when carrying one wasn't automatic. But then the last of the group arrived, Pete, the youngest of our crew. He'd seen us all leave our cell phones in the car and decided to bring his. A Nokia brick. Monochrome screen. No GPS.

He called 911 at 3:47 PM. "Where are you?" the dispatcher asked.

"I don't know," Pete said, his voice laced with the panic we were all feeling. "None of us know."

The dispatcher couldn't figure out where we were. Pete was surrounded by identical looking trees at the park, trying to explain where a service road was to a dispatcher miles away.

That's when things got weird. I never saw her myself. My memories from that time are just disconnected flashes of pain and light. This is what my friends told me.

They all agreed on a few things. She came out of nowhere, moving fast. Really fast. She took the phone from Pete, calm and authoritative, gave the dispatcher our exact location. Trail markers or coordinates. Without her, the ambulance would have been driving in circles. Then she grabbed a bike and took off to alert the park ranger.

The timeline made no sense. She was back almost immediately. The fire department showed up. They had to cut a lock to get to the trails. The DNR arrived with a pickup truck. Everything happened at once, and she just disappeared. Nobody saw where she went.

My friends all described her differently—except they all agreed she had long dark hair. No way I'll ever know the truth. All I know is that I'm still here.

Meanwhile, Nick had reached me first. Marc took off his shirt and used it to hold me down, working to stop me from bleeding. David took off on foot to scout ahead and guide the fire department to our exact location.

My memories from that point are just surreal, disconnected flashes. They came back, put me on a backboard, neck brace, strapped me down. The spinning red gumdrop light of the DNR pickup truck. Heavy Velcro straps across my chest, hips, legs. Foam blocks taped around my ears so I couldn't move my head even a millimeter. Staring straight up. As the truck bounced over the trail, the red beacon spun in tight circles. Every few seconds, red light swept across my face and the tree branches overhead. Dizzying strobe effect in the fading afternoon light. Movement without control. Voices that seemed far away even though people were right next to me.

I was out of my body. I would groan and moan in pain but couldn't make sense of what was going on.

As the firefighters and paramedics put me in the bed of the pickup and rushed me to the waiting ambulance, my buddies grabbed the bikes and headed to my car. Loaded everything up and hauled ass to chase the ambulance to the hospital for the ten mile trip. That's when they realized they better call my family. The only number anyone had was for my younger brother. They called him.

My brother then called my mom, which was unusual for him. Asked my parents how their night was going. They said they were on their way home from dinner. He said, "Well, Tom is unconscious being rushed to the hospital," then gave my buddy's phone number to get more details.

My mom and dad beat the ambulance to the hospital. She talks about how long the time took to go by, pacing outside the ER entrance. I remember seeing the big red EMERGENCY sign for a split second.

In the ambulance on the way to the hospital, I came to for a few seconds. Looked around. Looked at one of the paramedics and said, "Thank you for taking time out of your day to stop and pick me up, I greatly appreciate it." Then passed right back out. The paramedics told me later they lost it laughing. My politeness in the middle of serious trauma made their day, if not their entire career.

I woke up properly in the ER, wearing a neck brace, strapped to a backboard where I'd stay for hours waiting for an MRI. Heavy-duty molded plastic padded with stiff grey foam. When they cinched the Velcro straps, it felt like a cold hand gripping my throat. Tight enough I could feel my own pulse against the foam. The top of the brace was like a shelf for my chin. Every time I tried to swallow, my jaw pressed down into hard plastic. I couldn't move my head. Had to stare at the ceiling tiles. The foam covered my ears and wrapped under my jaw. My own breathing sounded loud. The plastic creaked when

I shifted. Everything outside sounded muffled, like listening through water.

Smell of antiseptic mixed with something metallic. Cold alcohol. Iodine. The copper smell of my own blood. Monitors beeping in different rhythms. High-pitched chirp of the pulse monitor. Squeak of rubber soles on linoleum. Low hum of the MRI machine.

After an hour, the area under the foam started sweating. The plastic didn't breathe. Heat from my neck stayed trapped. Created this deep, maddening itch I couldn't reach.

At one point, I offered my life savings to anyone who would take me off that board. The discomfort was unbearable. After hours, the plastic felt fused to my spine. My brain couldn't process the injury, only the desperate need to get unstrapped.

Eventually my mom was there. Talking to me. Concerned. Curious until she could see for herself. They asked me to wiggle my toes, press against their hand with my feet. When I moved my legs, the tension in her shoulders just collapsed. Her eyes welled up. She'd been thinking I might be paralyzed.

My first clear thought was, "Oh, that's why I've been asleep. Something happened."

I was laughing. It all made sense why things were fuzzy.

I had some memory loss. The hospital ER thought I was on a motorcycle.

Then friends and family kept coming to talk to me, check on me. I don't remember any conversations. I only know their side of the stories. I remember talking to Shane and Nick, hearing a loud groan of pain, then looking around, asking them, "Who the fuck did that? That was fucking loud. Who the fuck did that?" My brain was processing the sound as external, not my own voice. They tried to explain it was me, but I didn't get it. They couldn't stop laughing. I was all kinds of ridiculous.

The hospital got me into an MRI and a bunch of other tests. It's all a blur. I thanked my friends a billion times for helping me out of the woods between the tests.

When everything was said and done, at 3:33 AM the hospital decided I was okay enough to go home, but I wasn't to go outdoors since it was a hot summer for at least a week.

Word of the accident spread quickly through our circle. I sent an email to work with a picture from the ER saying see you in at least a week. This resulted in a bunch of people sending similar pictures back of when they got hurt on bikes.

I got to bed and had a few close friends stay over to keep watch over me. Then after a few days, more and more people came to visit. Various friends came over. People brought food. Coworkers, friends, extended family. It was great to talk to people.

In the hospital, the road rash across my face and shoulder started burning. A nurse came over with a basin of cold saline and stacks of gauze. First touch was a shocking chill that turned into sharp, white hot sting. I could hear the wet, sticky sound of the gauze as they scrubbed black asphalt grit and trail dirt out of the raw skin. Rhythmic and agonizing. Scrub, flush, repeat. Every time cold water hit the road burn, my breath hitched. The metallic smell of blood mixed with sharp chemical antiseptic. By the time they finished, my face felt twice its normal size, radiating steady, pulsing heat.

My face was super creepy to look at. Scrapes and scars along the top and down my side. When I go to a pool or water park, the scars show up more clearly after being in the water for a bit. People always ask questions. But to me, scars tell a story.

When I finally got back to work, I found helmets sitting on my desk. Brand-new, still in boxes with tags. On top was a letter from the CTO who led the entire IT department. He didn't start with "I'm sorry you got hurt." He started with a dry, self deprecating story about his own bike crash a few months before. It was funny but formal. The kind of letter that acknowledges a serious scare with a wink. He wrote about helmet safety and gave me a formal warning to stay upright. It felt good. Like I was part of a group that looked out for its own.

The Giro helmet I'd been wearing was beat up. Giant scrape down the side where the plastic wore down to foam. The outer shell had a deep, jagged gouge where it skidded across the road. Underneath, the white foam was crushed flat. That crush saved my life. The foam took the hit so my skull didn't have to.

I'm always wearing a helmet now. I don't feel comfortable without it. My buddies and I created a mountain bike team called the Helmet Heads. We used to raise helmet awareness on a regular basis, bike for the American Diabetes Association along with the Multiple Sclerosis Society.

Pete who happened to bring his first cell phone on the one day we'd need it most. The paramedics who remembered a polite patient. The friends who showed up at the hospital and every day during recovery. The coworkers who turned safety into kindness with a desk full of helmets.

The woman who appeared exactly when we needed her, gave the dispatcher our location, and then vanished.

2-5:
THE SHORTEST DISTANCE
(2016-2017)

By 2016, I was finally learning something I'd never been good at: leaving work at work. The healthcare system job was solid, stable, the kind of position where you could clock out at 5 PM and stop thinking about it. After years of being on call 24/7, of having my phone constantly demanding attention, this felt good.

I'd been there a few years. Stable and predictable.

I'd found a roommate on Craigslist. Adam, an automotive engineer looking to split rent on a townhouse near the data center where I worked. It seemed practical. Cut costs, have some company, maybe make a friend.

Adam was a super smart engineer who does what he enjoys. But more than that, he was so chill to talk to.

He got me playing online multiplayer games with my brother and friends. A few hours every few days where we could go into battle together, work something out of our systems, be guys doing stupid, fun, competitive things without any real-world consequences. It was exactly what I needed.

He also introduced me to competitive go-karting.

Adam thought about the world in terms of physics equations and optimal trajectories. While I was troubleshooting networks and fixing servers, he was analyzing suspension geometry and calculating tire adhesion. His approach to everything, from choosing the fastest route to work to organizing the kitchen for maximum efficiency, was methodical.

The local go-kart league met at an indoor track every few weeks, and he convinced me to join. Partly for the competition and partly because he thought I'd appreciate the technical aspects of finding speed through precision rather than raw power.

The league was an advanced physics seminar disguised as recreational racing.

The league was populated almost entirely by automotive engineers, professional test drivers, and people who designed suspension systems for major manufacturers. These weren't casual weekend racers looking for an adrenaline rush. They were professionals who understood vehicle dynamics at a level that made every lap an exercise in applied mathematics.

Before each race, we'd suit up in the lobby area. Full-face helmets, mandatory. Not the half-shell helmets you might wear on a bicycle. These were high-end racing helmets with visors that covered your entire face. Most of us wore mirrored visors. Dark smoke shields that made it impossible to see anything behind them.

When that visor clicked down with a sharp clack, the person vanished. You weren't racing Dave from Suspension Engineering. You were racing Kart #14.

It was like poker.

You couldn't read anyone's face. Couldn't see who was confident or nervous or calculating their next move. Couldn't see who was smiling behind that visor or gritting their teeth. Everyone was anonymous, reduced to their driving and their kart number.

Without facial expressions to read, you had to watch body lean. The way a helmet tilted toward the apex. How shoulders tensed right before a defensive move. You had to rely entirely on track position and driving behavior to understand who you were racing against. Was that aggressive move at turn three desperation or strategy? Was that defensive line someone protecting position or struggling with pace? You couldn't know. You had to respond and figure it out in real time.

For the first several months, I was consistently mid-pack. Fourth place, fifth place, occasionally third if someone ahead of me made a mistake or had mechanical problems. I was driving as hard as I could, taking risks that felt significant to me, pushing what seemed like the limits.

It was fun and easy. It didn't bother me. I was having fun. I didn't care if I won.

But I was missing something fundamental that everyone else seemed to understand intuitively.

The indoor track was tight, technical, designed to reward precision over raw speed. The air smelled like warm rubber and ozone from the electric motors. The karts were electric, which meant no roar of engines to communicate what the driver ahead was doing. Just a high-frequency electronic whine that rose and fell in pitch. It sounded like a jet engine. The squeal of tires on polished concrete. You learned to read the sound of tires. The chirp when the rear wheels slipped. The scrub, a low, grainy sound when you turned the wheel too sharp and killed your momentum.

Each lap felt like a puzzle to solve. The apex of turn three, where the track banked slightly and you could carry more speed than seemed possible. The chicane after the long straight where everyone braked too early or too late. The final hairpin that set you up for the fastest part of the track.

The karts themselves were surprisingly responsive. Electric motors have instant torque. The moment you touched the pedal, it didn't rev up. It just launched. An electric punch that kicked you in the back. You had to learn to roll onto the throttle so you didn't just spin the tires on that polished concrete. A twitch of the wheel, a slight adjustment in weight distribution, and you could feel the whole machine respond. When you got it right, there was a flow to it, a rhythm where each turn fed into the next. When you got it wrong, you'd scrub speed, lose momentum, watch the gap to the kart ahead open up.

After each race, they'd call us up for the podium ceremony. First, second, third. A small raised platform at the edge of the track. A carpeted riser. You'd stand there with your heart still racing, hair helmet-flat and sweaty, looking at guys who design suspension systems for a living. They'd hand you a small trophy or certificate, take a photo for their social media. It should have felt silly, grown men celebrating go-kart races like they'd won the Monaco Grand Prix.

But standing up there, even in third place, helmet off, feeling the cool air-conditioned lobby air hit your damp forehead, knowing you'd been racing against engineers who designed actual race cars, it felt earned. Every position was fought for. Every tenth of a second mattered.

What got me was standing below that podium, watching others celebrate, knowing I had the capability to be up there more consistently. I didn't know how yet.

The breakthrough came during a conversation after one particularly frustrating race where I'd been fast in practice but couldn't maintain that pace when it mattered. Adam asked me to describe my approach to a specific corner, a tight left-hander that led onto the longest straight section of the track.

As I explained my technique, he started sketching on a napkin, drawing the racing line I was describing versus the line he was taking. His pen moved across the napkin. A few simple ink lines. The difference was subtle but significant. Maybe two feet at the apex of the corner, a slightly different entry angle, a different point where he started his turn-in.

"Back in the pit area, he pulled out his phone and scrubbed through my GoPro footage.

'There.' He paused on a frame. 'You're turning in too early. See how tight you are against the inside? You're losing speed on exit.'

He pulled up his own footage from the same corner. His kart stayed wide on approach, turned in later, clipped the apex further around the bend. The speed difference on exit was obvious.

'Late apex,' he said. 'You want the shortest distance after the corner, not through it.'"

Seeing the lines on the paper. Going for the shortest point to point instead of how you drive on the road following your lane.

It made it all make so much sense.

The racing line wasn't about taking the shortest distance through individual corners. It was about finding the sequence of arcs and straight lines that minimized lap time by maximizing the amount of time spent at high speed. Sometimes this meant taking a longer path through a corner to set up a better exit onto a straight section. It felt like you were taking a longer path, but because you were straightening the exit, you could get back on that instant electric power five feet sooner than anyone else. In a twelve-turn race, that's sixty feet of advantage per lap. Sometimes it meant sacrificing speed in one corner to improve your position for the next three.

Every choice affected the next three corners. The goal wasn't to be fast in any individual moment, but to be efficient across the complete circuit.

I stopped trying to muscle the kart through corners or find speed through aggression. Started focusing on precision. Studied the lines the faster drivers were taking. Began to see why they were doing things that initially seemed counterintuitive.

The improvement wasn't immediate. Changing fundamental techniques while racing requires overriding instincts that have been developing through practice. But gradually, my lap times began dropping. More importantly, my consistency improved. Instead of having one or two fast laps per race with several slower ones mixed in, I could maintain a steady pace that was competitive throughout an entire session.

The podium started feeling more familiar. Third became consistent. Second became possible. First happened once, and the photograph they took that day showed me grinning like an idiot, helmet in hand.

Behind those visors, you couldn't see anyone else grinning. But I knew they were. We were all competing against each other, but we were also all competing against the track itself, against physics, against our own ability to execute the perfect lap.

Shane, Marc, and Greg showed up at the same track a few months later. My friends from DECA. Guys I'd known since high school, the ones who'd taught me about cars back then.

I watched Shane dive into turn three. He was doing exactly what I used to do: hugging the inside, taking the shortest distance through the corner. Fast and confident, but his kart scrubbed speed on exit.

'You're quick in there,' I said when he came back to the pit.

'Yeah, but you're pulling away on the straights,' he said. 'What am I missing?'

I grabbed a napkin and drew the line. 'Try starting wider. Turn in later. Clip the apex here instead of here.'

He looked skeptical but tried it his next session. Came back nodding.

The difference was immediately apparent. While they were fighting the karts and each other, making the tires scream in protest, I was racing the track itself. Flowing. Using the smallest possible steering inputs to maintain the highest possible velocity. Finding speed through efficiency rather than effort.

When they accused me of having a faster kart or some kind of mechanical advantage, I tried to explain. "It's the lines," I told them, sketching racing paths on whatever surface was available.

I won that race by a margin that surprised everyone, including myself.

I wasn't braver than them. I was just more efficient.

It was math.

I thought I hated math.

2-6:
HOUSE HUNTING
(2008)

By 2008, all the adults in my life had started saying the same thing.

"You must be making decent money now." "A house is the best investment you can make." "They aren't making anymore land." "When are you gonna buy a house?"

The old timers at work. Family friends. People who looked at me like I was wasting my twenties if I wasn't building equity. Not one person asked me what I wanted.

After winning Intern of the Year at the marketing company, they offered me a full time position. I accepted. By 2008, I was making decent money. The pressure was constant.

I started looking at houses. Touring them on weekends. Walking through strangers' personal decisions turned into real estate. Some of those decisions were deeply weird.

There was one house that had two garages. Seemed promising. Then I saw one of them had been built directly over an in-ground swimming pool. Not beside it. Not near it. Over it. The pool was still there. Empty. In dire need of repairs. A normal ranch home. Maybe a thousand square feet. Nothing looked strange until you went to the backyard and saw two garages. Why would someone do this?

Another house was sixteen hundred square feet of purple carpet and mirrors everywhere. I mean everywhere. Mirrors on the walls. Mirrors on the ceiling. Mirrored tiles running down the hallways. The power was off when I toured it. I was walking through this maze with a flashlight. The beam bouncing off surfaces in disorienting ways. In one corner of what might have once been a bedroom, I found a dead bird lying on the purple carpet. I left quickly.

Then there was the hearts house. Seven hundred fifty square feet. Hearts everywhere. On the walls. The cabinets. Painted on the floors. Someone had committed to a theme. It smelled like fresh cookies when I walked in. Homey. But ridiculous.

I saw a house with a carpeted bathroom. The whole thing. Floor. Walls around the tub. Even a little wall around the toilet. That's for older people so they don't slip and fall. Made sense. Still looked weird.

I saw over fifty homes. Houses with kitchens designed by people who never cooked. Houses where every room was painted a different primary color. Walking through all of them thinking this one doesn't get it. None of them got it.

Then I found one I actually wanted. Corner house with a detached garage. Workshop space. Unfinished basement. Hardwood floors. Brick. Simple. Reasonably priced.

I got my brother there ahead of time. We hid him inside before my parents came to look at it with me. My brother and I had this alliance. We'd scare my mom. It was our thing. We'd been told after the Bowling Night Ambush that we were no longer allowed to scare mom on purpose. But this opportunity was too good.

The house was an empty shell, which meant every sound was loud. The hardwood floors made every footstep echo. The kitchen was quiet, smelling of dust and the faint hint of hearts wallpaper. My brother was folded into the dark pantry, the air inside smelling like old shelf liner and stale wood.

My mom's footsteps on the oak floor as she walked through the tour. When she reached the kitchen, the air was still. Then came the prolonged creak of the pantry door hinges.

He jumped out. The scream wasn't just a noise. It was an event that bounced off the bare plaster walls and high ceilings. The laughter that followed from me, my brother, and my dad was the first real life that house had seen in a year. My mom would be jumpy all the time after that. It was very easy to make her jump. That was part of playing.

I got outbid on that house.

The search continued through all the seasons. Spring. Summer heat. Fall leaves turning. Then I found it.

I pulled into the driveway. Double wide closer to the garage. Perfect for extra parking. Then single wide as it worked its way down. Easier to shovel in winter. Half acre lot. Twenty three thousand square feet of yard space. The brick ranch sat on it like it had always been there. There was a big pine tree out front. And a birch tree with white bark that caught the afternoon light.

Nine hundred twenty five square feet on the main floor. Three bedrooms. Partially finished basement with another two hundred square feet. Small. But it would be mine.

I walked in and the first thing I saw was the living room. Eighteen by thirteen. Big picture window looking out to the backyard. Lots of natural light. Little closet by the door for coats. The kitchen was sixteen by ten. Outdated but in good shape. The cabinets were solid.

When I first turned the key, the air was heavy. Not a bad smell, just the scent of a house that had been sitting empty. Frozen in time. The hearts wallpaper wasn't just a pattern. It was a commitment. Tiny, repetitive red and pink hearts marched across every wall.

Down the hall were three bedrooms. The master was twelve by eleven. Looked out to the backyard. Had the biggest window and the biggest closet. Guest bedroom was eleven by ten. The third bedroom was ten by nine. That would become my office. My tech lab. Had windows. Every room had windows. I loved all the natural light. There was not one door you could close without a window allowing in the sunlight.

One full bathroom. One half bath. The full bathroom had hearts wallpaper. The basement was partially finished. Carpeted steps going down. Detached two car garage with workshop space. The house had been vacant for a year. Frozen in time. Free of life.

The decision was made quickly. Paperwork. Inspections. Financing. Within a few weeks I had keys in my hand. Most people didn't find out I was even looking until I had the keys. There was something satisfying about that. Making a major life decision quietly.

Move in day was simple. I used the mini van. Just had a bed. A couple little couches. A few other things. Nick was there. My brother too. The three of us were almost done by the time my parents showed up with lunch. Done in an afternoon.

That first night I couldn't sleep. It was maybe one in the morning. I'd spent most of the night organizing. I took all my possessions. Everything I owned. Laid them out in the house. The bed in the master bedroom. The little couches in the living room. A couple things scattered around.

Then I sat in each room. Just sitting. Staring. Daydreaming about what to do with it. What could go here. What that space could become. How I'd use each room. The house was mine. Empty. Full of possibility.

I went to Home Depot the next day to look at paint samples. Walked through the color section. Then I found the oops paint section. The paint they'd mixed wrong for other people. Dirt cheap. I bought some.

My bedroom became Kelly Green. The bathroom baby poop brown. Kitchen sky blue. Living room radical red.

The living room was eighteen by thirteen. When I started, it was a hollow white box. The radical red oops paint was thick, heavy, and smelled like a fresh chemical spill. As I rolled the first strip onto the center of the wall, the contrast was violent. It looked like wet blood against the sterile white. It was thick and uneven. It didn't just cover the wall. It ate it.

It took three full coats to get an even finish. By the third pass, the room stopped being a vacant space and started feeling real. The sunlight hitting that red wall in the afternoon didn't just light the room. It made the air itself seem to glow. My forearms were splattered with red dots, and the muscles in my shoulder burned from the repetitive motion of the roller.

One wall in the kitchen I turned into a giant chalkboard wall. It became the message center for parties. Friends wrote each other notes. People drew. The sound of the chalk snapping and the white dust that would settle on the kitchen floor after a party. It was awesome.

Later that night I was lying on my bed in the master bedroom. Just me and empty rooms. The house was so quiet. No traffic sounds. No neighbors. Just the settling sounds of an old house adjusting to having someone in it again after sitting vacant for a year. The wood floorboards would pop as they cooled down. The rhythmic ticking of the copper pipes in the basement.

I was almost asleep when I felt it.

A hand. On my foot. Through the blanket. Firm. Deliberate. Like someone was checking if I was awake.

I froze.

My eyes shot open. I stared at the ceiling. The streetlight outside cast shadows through the window. Tree branches moving in whatever wind existed.

The grip was still there.

I yanked my foot back. Sat up. Looked at the end of the bed. Nothing.

The room was empty. The door was closed. The windows were closed. Just me and the furniture I'd moved in that afternoon.

My heart was pounding. I could feel it in my chest. In my throat. In my ears.

I sat there for what felt like forever. Listening. Watching. Waiting for something else to happen.

Nothing did.

I got out of bed. Walked through every room. Turned on every light. Checked every closet. Every door. Every window. Everything was locked. Everything was exactly where I'd left it.

Maybe I'd imagined it. Maybe it was my foot falling asleep and my brain making up a story. Maybe the house settling had vibrated the bed frame in just the right way. Maybe I was exhausted from moving.

Maybe.

I called Marc. Talked to him for a while. He helped me calm down. Asked if I wanted him to come over. I said no. I was fine. Just tired. Just adjusting.

The next morning I met my neighbor with the hedge. Not the electrician. The other one. She mentioned that someone had died in that house.

I didn't tell her about the night before.

I still don't know what happened. I felt what I felt.

If you asked me if I believe in ghosts, I'm not sure I could answer you.

A few friends came over to see the house. They walked through. Checked out the rooms. Complimented the paint colors. Then they opened my fridge.

Empty.

They checked the cabinets.

Also empty.

"When are you going to get staples?" one of them asked.

"What's that?"

They looked at each other. Then they took me to the grocery store.

Rice. Pasta. Flour. Potatoes. Olive oil. Canola oil. Vinegar. Butter. Onions. Garlic. Salt. Pepper. Canned tomatoes. Beans. Stock. Soy sauce. Honey. Eggs. Lemons.

The cart filled up fast.

"This is what normal people have in their kitchen," they explained. *"So you can actually cook something without going to the store every single time."*

We got back to the house. Loaded everything into the cabinets and fridge. Suddenly the kitchen looked like a kitchen.

They also made me get bathroom stuff. A plunger. Extra toilet paper. Even tampons.

"You don't need tampons," I said.

"Your guests might."

That made sense.

They put together what they called a hospitality kit. Fresh roll of toilet paper. Variety pack of tampons and pads. Air freshener. All in a small basket under the sink.

"This is what grown-ups do," one of them said.

During my first week, I found a garage sale a few blocks over. They had an air hockey table. A pool table. A foosball table. The guy running the sale looked tired. Like he just wanted it all gone.

"How much for all three?"

He quoted me a price. I had a truck. We loaded them up.

Getting them into the house was the hard part. The foosball table was the easiest to move. My brother and I got that one inside. It went in the garage.

The air hockey table was manageable. My brother and one of his friends helped me carry it to the basement.

The pool table was different. That thing was so heavy. The three of us tried to angle it through the basement door. We got it partway down the stairs and it just stopped. Wedged. We couldn't push it down. Couldn't pull it back up.

We stood there sweating. Trying to figure out the angles. Trying different ways to move it.

Before we knew it, neighbors were walking into the house. The electrician from next door. His two neighbors. They made easy work of the pool table.

They just showed up and started helping. No introduction. No asking if we needed it. They saw us struggling through the window and came over.

With everyone working together, we got the pool table unstuck. Maneuvered it down the stairs. Set it up in the basement.

A riding lawn mower would be good for a half acre lot. I found one on a message board a few hours north in the country. Drove up to get it.

It was my favorite. You had to pop the hood after turning the key and touch wires together to start it. The moment the metal touched, there was a sharp, blue white flash. A miniature bolt of lightning that left a purple spot in my vision for a second. There was a distinct crack sound, and then the heavy whir whir thump of the starter motor.

When the engine finally caught, the entire chassis would shudder. I could feel the vibration travel from the soles of my boots, up through my legs, and into my chest. The roar of the engine was loud, dangerous, and completely satisfying.

It had no safety features. None. If you got off with it in gear, it would keep going.

First time mowing, I hopped off to move a branch. The mower just kept driving. Straight toward the garage. I had to run after it and jump back on. My neighbors were in their yards watching. Laughing. I waved like it was all part of the plan.

So much fun learning how to do yard work.

I also had no idea how to do laundry. The first load I did, I pulled my jeans out of the dryer and held them against my chest to carry them upstairs. The metal button was still hot from the dryer. It pressed right under my chin. Burned me. Left a perfect circular print. A branded circle.

I stood there in the laundry room looking at myself in the mirror. Button shaped burn under my chin. The stinging sensation when I touched it.

Still learning.

My family and friends now had a place to take things that were too good to throw away and they didn't want anymore.

My aunt showed up one day with a floor lamp. "I thought you could use this."

My mom brought over dishes. Pots and pans. A microwave.

Friends dropped off furniture. A chair. A bookshelf. Random kitchen gadgets.

Before I knew it, the house was full. Every room had something in it. The empty space filled up fast.

One Saturday afternoon I was in the driveway working on something. I don't even remember what. The electrician from next door came over.

"You doing okay?" he asked.

"Yeah. Good."

He nodded. Looked at what I was doing. Offered a suggestion. Then went back to his yard.

Ten minutes later the other neighbor was out. Waved. Asked if I needed anything.

That's how it was. The neighbors were always around. Always watching. Always taking care of each other.

2-7:
THE SHERIFF'S SALE
(2012)

The house was far more than I could afford. One of my two monthly paychecks went entirely to the mortgage, leaving the other to cover every single other bill and expense in my life. For four and a half years, I lived in a constant state of being underwater.

My life shrank to a single loop. Going to work, going home. There was no money for anything extra. No dinners out, no spontaneous adventures, no margin for the unexpected expenses that make life livable. I survived off manager's special food from the grocery store. Bright yellow and orange stickers marking down the bruised produce and meat nearing its expiration date.

It didn't bother me. Sometimes I'd eat things that were already past their date.

One day I went to the manager's special section and the only thing there was a collection of beef marrow bones, wrapped in plastic on a foam tray for a dollar each. I bought all of them, took them home, and put them on a cookie sheet with a little salt and pepper. I didn't know what I was doing, but I knew one rule. If you want to make something good, cook it low and slow.

After at least an hour, I pulled them out. As I worked to get the small bits of marrow from the middle of the bones, I started laughing at the ridiculousness of it all. "No wonder these things were on clearance," I thought. "Who does this?"

And then I tasted it.

Fatty, buttery texture that melted on my tongue. A deep, rich flavor that felt primal and essential. My body was literally plugging into a power source it had been missing for months. I had a single, clear thought. Wow, my body needs this.

I often still had friends over on Sunday nights no matter what, even though most weeks it was simple spaghetti and pasta sauce with lots of garlic. If I couldn't have happiness, I could have garlic, which is the same thing.

The shower curtain in my bathroom was ripped. It was a simple, five-dollar fix, but even that felt like a luxury I couldn't afford. I kept patching it together with duct tape.

One night, standing in that bathroom looking at that duct-taped shower curtain, I felt the frustration wash over me.

My parents knew I was struggling, even though I was too proud to ask for help directly. Sometimes I'd come home from work to find things magically fixed or replaced. A new shower curtain appeared one day, a bag of groceries on the counter another. It was a silent, loving intervention.

I was touched. They always know what's going on.

At the law firm, I was a digital forensics professional. Hard drives, evidence processing, write blockers. No food in the lab. The breakroom became my staging area.

I would skip eating until I got to the office. The snack cabinet saved me more than I wish to admit. Ramen noodle cups, Nature Valley Oats 'n Honey granola bars, fruit snacks, mixed nuts, various chips. My go-to was those granola bars. The ones that shatter into a thousand jagged crumbs the moment you open the wrapper. Shrapnel.

I developed a system. I'd step out of the lab and head to the breakroom. Take two rough, brown industrial paper towels from the dispenser and tuck them into my collar, draping them across my chest like a bib. Snap the bar while it was still in the green plastic sleeve to contain the initial blast, then carefully consume the shards over the sink.

Five minutes later, the bib was gone, the crumbs were swept away, and I was back in the lab. No one knew my lunch was a free granola bar and a paper towel apron.

The breaking point came from an unlikely source. A late-night TV commercial promising a "fresh start" through bankruptcy. Sitting in my empty living room at 2 AM, watching some lawyer promise that there was a way out, I decided to go for it.

I didn't ask for help or advice. I hired the first attorney I found, who turned out to be terrible. To them, I was a dollar in their bank account. I had been super hard on myself with my paperwork, expecting someone to review it carefully, to push back on my harsh self-assessment. But they didn't even look at it. They processed me through like any other case.

Because I made too much money for a Chapter 7 bankruptcy, I was put on a punishing Chapter 13 plan that left me with $600 a month to cover fuel, insurance, car payment, food, and utility bills. During the colder months, my utility bills would jump to $300 or more. Heat wasn't optional in a Michigan winter.

I wasn't going outside much anyway, except to shovel snow off the sidewalks. The city ordinance required me to clear from one end of my property line to the other, which meant shoveling my neighbor's section too. The sidewalk was only in front of our two houses. If I didn't clear the whole thing, I'd get a ticket. So there I was, broke, hungry, and exhausted, clearing a neighbor's sidewalk just to avoid a fine from a city that was essentially fining me for being neighborly. I just found it funny.

When utilities spiked in winter, I would have to skip eating. Not skip a meal here or there. Skip eating for days at a time.

My friend Brian connected me with an attorney named Elizabeth. She asked to be called Elizabeth, not Ms. anything. Just Elizabeth. It was her way of saying she was part of my tribe for this fight.

She was professional and to the point. She didn't need to know my story to justify anything. She could see it all in the paperwork.

She took one look at my disastrous paperwork with her legal pad and high-quality pen, shook her head, and went back to court. She managed to get the financial pressure reduced enough to give me breathing room.

I felt like things were starting to look up.

The very first thing I did with my newfound freedom was order Chinese food. It had been years since I'd had takeout.

The plastic bag crinkled as I set it on the counter. The styrofoam hinges popped and squeaked as I opened the container. Steam hit my face, carrying the sharp, sweet scent of ginger, dried red chilies, and soy. The smell of a world that was open to me again.

The crispy, fried exterior of the chicken gave way to the tender middle. It wasn't low and slow marrow. It was immediate gratification.

I cracked open the fortune cookie. The slip of paper read: "The most reliable way to predict the future is to engineer it yourself."

I stuck it on the fridge next to the foreclosure notice.

Almost another year passed.

It was a Wednesday. I got home around eight.

I saw the white paper from the driveway. Folded in half. Heavy-duty clear packing tape holding it to the door by where I parked.

I knew what it was.

I pulled up. Got out of the car. Walked to the door and read it standing there.

NOTICE OF MORTGAGE FORECLOSURE SALE in big letters across the top. Below that, the legal language. Default has been made in the conditions of a mortgage. The amount due. The sale date. The address of my house written out in official terms like it belonged to someone else.

Thirty days to vacate.

I peeled the tape off. The sound echoed in the quiet Wednesday night. Folded it back up. Went inside.

Put it on the fridge with a magnet.

The thing had no value to me. My attorney had planned all of this. It wasn't a surprise.

It was time for everything to change again.

I looked at my list of next living places. Started setting up apartment tours.

I saw two or three before finding the one. It was just under a mile from work. Had central AC. Cement floors between the floors so it would be super quiet. A carport.

The landlord met me there. An older woman. High energy. The apartment was empty. Fresh paint. New carpet.

She took me to the leasing office to sign the paperwork. Another apartment that wasn't being used as an apartment. The walls were lined with mirrors. Floor-to-ceiling, gold and silver trim. A relic of 1970s glam design. It felt like walking into a funhouse.

As she moved and spoke, I could see myself reflected from every angle. Ten versions of me signing ten copies of the paperwork.

I complimented them.

"Don't install mirrors like these," she said. *"The person who rented this before got fined when they moved out. But I loved them so I kept them."*

I found that fascinating.

I signed the lease. Timed the move-in for two weeks before my thirty-day deadline. Gave myself plenty of room.

I was already packing by this point. Planning to be out weeks before I was required.

A few days passed before the weekend when move-in day started.

I had more people show up than I expected. Six cars. Three pickups. One utility trailer.

I put them into teams. Kitchen. Electronics. Garage. Furniture. It worked great.

They didn't help. They organized. I had sorted my life into boxes, and they descended on the house. In what felt like no time, the house was empty.

When we got to my new one-bedroom apartment, Ruby, one of the women on the crew, had a stroke of genius. The new apartment was behind a local grocery store, and they ran over and grabbed a fleet of shopping carts. Heavy wire-mesh carts. We formed a brigade, loading the carts and rolling them right to my front door. The rattle-clack-clack of the metal wheels over the concrete and sidewalk joints. It sounded like efficiency.

The entire move took about three hours. Afterward, we all went out to dinner and had a great time, laughing and celebrating.

Move-in day was also the anniversary of my bike accident. Same day my contract position at the healthcare company converted to full-time.

It's one of those days.

I had fifteen to twenty bicycles in the garage. I picked my favorite three and my unicycles to move with me. The rest I took to the curb one at a time. I'd leave one, walk back to the garage, and by the time I returned with the next, the first was gone. A silent conversation with my neighbors. I was clearing the weight of the last four years and providing a fleet for the neighborhood. When I figured out which neighbor was taking them, I just brought the rest of the pile over to his house.

A few days later, the bank called. There were materials in the basement. Flooring. A few sheets of plywood. Nothing crazy. They came with the house when I bought it, but now the bank said they were forbidden. I'd be fined if I didn't remove them.

They left the door unlocked for me to go back and take care of it.

I dragged it all to the curb. Someone would grab it soon enough.

By day, corporate IT infrastructure, high-security badges, the kind of job where you're invisible when everything works and blamed when it doesn't.

By night and weekends, something else entirely.

For six years, I thought I was managing the balance.

3-1:
THE KINDNESS OF STRANGERS
(2006)

I was driving my truck to work when I heard a sharp, violent pop. The truck immediately started pulling hard to the right. Leftovers from Gracie See's were sitting on the middle seat. That pizza place from the old neighborhood. I'd been looking forward to them all morning.

I managed to get over to the shoulder. I don't change tires on the shoulder. Too dangerous. But I knew my hand was getting forced.

I got out to look. The spare tire was held under the truck on a pulley. The pulley had rusted. Not just surface rust. The kind of rust that fuses metal together. The kind where you can't tell where one piece ends and another begins.

I was trying to figure out my approach when I heard a voice yell down from above.

"You need some help?"

I looked up. A man was standing on the embankment behind a beat-up chain-link fence.

I ignored him at first. In Detroit, you don't accept help. It's best to not make anyone's business your business.

"It's a rusty pulley," he called down. *"I've fixed many of them. Can I help?"*

I looked at the pulley again. Looked back up at him.

"Yeah," I called back. *"That would be amazing."*

He asked me to come up and hold the broken fence down so he could climb over. I climbed the hill and pressed down on the loose section while he hopped over.

His name was Vincent.

"Don't worry," he said as he walked toward my truck, reading the tension in my body language. *"I'm not going to shank you."*

I laughed. Nervous. But genuine. The directness of it was reassuring.

He got to work immediately.

Vincent fixed the rusty part I hadn't been able to manage on my own. Changed the tire with expert quickness. The kind of speed that comes from doing something a hundred times.

When he was done, I had a problem. I had no cash on me to offer him for his help.

I suggested taking him to an ATM.

At the drive-through, Vincent respectfully turned his back and waited for me to finish my transaction before I handed him some cash.

Then he asked if I could give him a ride to drop off the money for groceries at a friend's house. They would bring the groceries to him later.

"Of course," I said.

Vincent directed me into a neighborhood I didn't recognize.

This was a rough area of Detroit. The kind you don't want to be stopped in. Burnt-out houses stood next to decent ones. Charred window frames. Collapsed roofs. Then a house with a fresh coat of paint. Then another burned shell. The pattern repeated down every block.

That's when I saw the first barrier.

Concrete. The kind that's been there for years. Weathered. Stained. Positioned to force traffic into specific patterns. One way in. One way out.

"Turn left here," Vincent said.

I turned.

On the corner stood four men. All of them dressed in black and blue. Matching. They looked at my truck. Then at Vincent.

Vincent nodded.

They nodded back.

It was cold out. I was roasting warm.

"Right at the next street," Vincent said.

Another corner. Four more men. Same colors. Same watching. Same nod.

Vincent directed me deeper. Left here. Straight. Right there.

More barriers. More corners. More men in black and blue.

Each group watched us pass. Each time Vincent nodded. Each time they nodded back.

I was thinking about what caseload I'd see when I got to work. How late I was going to be. Whether I even needed coffee today.

I didn't understand how Vincent was getting groceries. Where was the store? Why were we driving so deep into a neighborhood?

But I kept driving. Following his directions.

I started counting turns. Trying to track where I was. Trying to map a way out in my head.

I lost count.

The neighborhood became a maze. Barriers forcing turns. Streets that looked the same. Corners with men watching. No through streets. No way to just drive straight and get out.

It had only been a few minutes.

It felt like half an hour.

"Turn here," Vincent said.

I turned onto a dead-end street.

"Pull up there and beep the horn three times."

I did as he asked.

Vincent looked at me. "Whatever you do," he said, "do not leave me."

My stomach dropped.

Before I could respond, Vincent got out of the truck and disappeared into a house.

I sat there. Engine running. Hands on the steering wheel.

A moment later, a silver sedan pulled up behind me. Blocked me in. No way to reverse. No way out.

Four men got out.

Large men. Moving with purpose. Walking toward my truck.

My body knew before my brain did.

Heart pounding. Hands locked on the steering wheel. Every muscle tensed. The cold sweat kind of fear. The kind that starts in your gut and floods outward until you can't think straight.

I was going to get robbed.

That's what this was. That's why Vincent brought me here. The maze. The barriers. The men on every corner. No way out. No witnesses. Just me and my truck in a dead-end street with four men walking toward me and Vincent gone.

I fucked up.

They were getting closer. Ten feet. Five feet.

I couldn't move. Couldn't think. Couldn't do anything but watch them approach through my windshield.

Three feet.

Pure muscle. All of them. The kind of build that comes from more than just working out. Faces I couldn't read. Moving with purpose.

Then Vincent yelled from a nearby porch. "Hey Tom! Don't worry about them, worry about this!"

A woman standing next to him pulled up her shirt and flashed me.

For a second.

The men stopped.

I turned to look at the porch.

For a few seconds, nothing happened. Time stretched. My brain couldn't process.

I wasn't getting hit. Nobody was opening my door. Nobody was reaching through my window.

I'd just seen a woman's chest.

That's what just happened.

The men looked at the porch. Then burst out laughing.

They got back in their car and drove away like the whole thing had been an elaborate joke.

Vincent got back in my truck. Still laughing.

I couldn't form words. My hands were still locked on the steering wheel. My brain was trying to catch up to what just happened.

The fear. The certainty I was about to be robbed. The men walking toward me. The flash. The laughter.

None of it made sense.

Then I started laughing too. Nervous. Confused. Terrified. But laughing.

We all laughed.

"I have no idea what just happened," I finally managed.

Vincent directed me back out of the neighborhood. Left here. Right there. Straight through.

I followed on autopilot.

The men on corners nodded as we passed. The same men who'd watched us drive in. The barriers that had felt like a trap on the way in now just looked like street furniture on the way out.

When we reached a main road I recognized, Vincent had me pull over at a gas station.

I sat there. Adrenaline still draining. Trying to make sense of it.

Normal traffic moving past. People pumping gas. The world going about its business like I hadn't just been terrified out of my mind.

I grabbed the Gracie See's container from the middle seat.

"Here," I said, handing it to Vincent. "Take this too."

He took it. Nodded. "Thanks for the ride," he said. "And for the help with the money."

"Thank you for changing my tire," I said. "Seriously."

Vincent smiled. "You're alright," he said.

Then he was gone.

I sat there for a while longer. Hands still shaking. Heart rate slowly coming back to normal.

I got to work three hours late that day.

3-2:
THE IMPOSSIBLE TASK
(2009-2011)

T he job interview had been unremarkable until I was about to leave. I looked at my future director's whiteboard and saw a list of software suites. I recognized one from my teenage years, something I'd used for research purposes. Network layout tools, ways of gathering information.

I asked some questions. Then suggested a few other options, ways of doing things with a read-only operating system so we could use devices for data collections with no risk of data being compromised.

He did a 180. We connected. It was like the days of dial-up modems making the connection, going faster and faster until both ends sync at the fastest speed they could detect.

I got the job.

The firm was in a giant high-rise in central metro Detroit. Beautiful building. Our suites were pretty, the kind of place that took care of their people. But you also had to work hard. There was a thrill to it. This was the job where impossible things could be done with technology.

This was the early start of the ediscovery division. I supported electronic discovery data center operations. I assisted forensic investigators remotely and in the field. The amounts of data to be stored across various kinds of disk, data that had to be quickly ingested and processed then moved to slower, cheaper storage for long term storage without breaking chain of custody.

I can't go into details. Most of this job is still best practice to treat as if it's under an NDA (non-disclosure agreement). My friends often thought I was a spy because I couldn't tell them what I was doing, how long I was doing it, or where I was going.

My director was a great man, wonderful to talk to. We would discuss ideas for hours. He'd assign me tasks that were impossible. Not difficult. Impossible based on what had been done anywhere in the world at that time. He'd tell me to keep trying anyway.

And eventually, I'd make it happen.

I loved sitting in people's offices, looking around, reverse engineering how they think in order to set up a database of possible passwords to start my brute force cracking. Rainbow Tables and massive wordlists. Every personal photo, every sports team logo, every detail told me something about how their mind worked, what they valued, what words they might use to protect their digital life. Kids' names. Pets. Birthdays. Anniversary dates. The human element of password security.

A few months into the job, I got sent to New York City on assignment. I couldn't tell anyone where I was going or why.

Not friends, not family, nobody. For years afterward, I couldn't say a thing, even though everyone wanted to know.

I was in NYC ten days at a time, then would switch with a counterpart. Ten days back home, then back to New York. We went back and forth for quite some time.

One of my first nights there, my mom called to see how my trip was going. I deflected to the plane ride, how I met a woman next to me, how cool it was to meet an author. I talked about everything except what I was doing.

She asked if I was in town for someone she saw on a national news channel.

I froze. I panicked. I saw how big this was and how keeping it a secret was a must. I couldn't lie to my mom.

I deflected again. I described the incredible bagels, the modern office, how we'd rented bicycles in the park on a beautiful spring day.

She tried one more time. I changed the subject.

She eventually let it go.

Earlier that day, when we'd landed in NYC, my director and I were picked up by a black car service. A Lincoln Town Car. One of those men in a suit holding a little sign with a name we were being called. They took us to a building. When we went inside, we had to sign in with a three-letter agency to enter a crime scene.

I didn't know why I was there, but I'd brought all the wires and equipment to handle anything I could think of. There was a TV on in the office, and it was showing a helicopter view of the building I was standing in. Live, real time. They were arresting someone accused of one of the biggest Ponzi schemes of that era.

This job was so exciting. The people were brilliant, supportive, pushing me to do the impossible and celebrating when I pulled it off.

But I was making so many sacrifices for that excitement.

I worked all hours of the day and night, constantly canceling plans for last minute projects. My phone was always on, always within reach, always demanding attention. I told myself it was worth it. The prestige, the challenge, the validation of being chosen for this elite team.

It was Good Friday, 2011, and the firm had declared a half day. I'd made plans to meet my aunts for lunch, a rare opportunity to spend time with family during daylight hours. I finished my assigned work, packed up my desk, and was about to leave when an investigator sent an email. He was leaving for the day, but the project had to be shipped out in time to make the other office by Monday morning.

Critical. Urgent. No one else could handle it.

I called my aunts and rescheduled for dinner.

Dinner time came, and more projects appeared. I could see the hours stretching ahead of me. I'd be lucky to leave by 9 PM to make the last FedEx pickup in the state. The hub at Detroit Metro Airport stayed open until 10 PM. I called again, apologized again, promised I'd call them in the morning for breakfast.

The next morning, I tried calling my one aunt. No answer. Called the other. No answer.

Then my phone rang. My mom's voice was wrong. Distraught.

"Your aunt had a heart attack last night."

I was already moving. I grabbed my work laptop and everything I might need if I got called, threw it all in the car, and started driving to the hospital. My hands were shaking on the steering wheel.

Fifteen minutes into the drive, I heard my work phone chirp. Just an email, I told myself. Ignore it.

Fifteen minutes later, my work phone rang.

My supervisor, asking if I could hop on a project.

"I can't," I said. *"I'm headed to the hospital. My aunt had a heart attack. Can you take care of it? I've got to go."*

There was a response. I don't remember what was said. It could have been good or bad. I was not in a state capable of work at that time.

I couldn't see my aunt at the hospital. Too many people, her kids were there. I went to her house. My other aunt showed up by chance, and we went for food.

A few weeks later, my aunt came home from the hospital. She survived the heart attack. I visited her and she told me something.

She looked me in the eye.

"Do it now," she said. *"Don't wait. Do the things you want to do. Make a big life."*

It took me months to process that. But I could see it now. The people sacrificing their love for their loved ones for a job. It was the right path for some. It wasn't the right thing for me.

It's time to change some things.

I handed in my notice a few months later. When I told my director, he wiped a tear from his eye. I'd been there from the beginning, one of the people who'd helped pioneer this work.

I'm gonna miss them. He was a great mentor to me.

But I'd gotten passed up for promotion. And after learning I was the lowest paid person on the entire team who worked all hours, I knew I couldn't stay.

I took what I thought was a significant pay cut to join a healthcare company. It turned out to be a raise in pay and half the hours. I'd been underpaid all along.

3-3:
THE BLACK HOLE
(2011-2013)

Walking into the healthcare company in December 2011 was a culture shock. After the frantic pace of the law firm, this new environment felt completely different.

There was so much space. The place was only IT people. Security was tight. You had to badge in and out of most things.

This wasn't just badge in at the door and you're good. This was Get Smart level security.

Seven badge swipes to get to the data center.

Seven.

The first swipe got you through the building entry into the man trap. A small room with a security window where you waited for the first door to close before the second would open. The heavy magnetic door would clunk shut behind you. Like an airlock. We called it the man trap and it felt exactly like that.

The second got you out of the man trap and into the main IT floor. Huge old school cubes. The kind where shorter coworkers could sneak around without you seeing them. Whiteboards everywhere.

The third got you into the secret hallway south. This is where it started feeling like a spy movie.

The fourth got you into the courtyard with generators.

The fifth got you into the secret hallway north. Fewer people. Quieter.

The sixth got you into the work room for server repairs and vendor access. Benches and tools and spare parts. Where vendors would work on equipment if it was new enough.

This was where I'd frankenstein systems back to life. Way more proper than anything I'd done before. This place was enterprise class everything.

The seventh and final swipe got you into the data center itself.

The building was kept cold. Everyone wore hoodies or kept dress coats at their desks. Some even had blankets.

I figured it out the first day when I arrived too hot and started to settle in to a new life.

But the data center? That was where the magic happened.

The first time I badged into the data center, the sound hit me before anything else. A sustained roar of cooling fans, like standing next to a jet engine that never quite took off. Thousands of blade servers in blade centers, stacked in racks. Imagine a video game cartridge from the Nintendo days, except these slid into the side of an enclosure. They could pop in and out, making it easy to work on individual components without disassembling everything. Their tiny high-RPM fans spinning at max speed.

Then the cold air hit my face. Even colder than the rest of the building. A brisk 62 degrees. Cold aisle temperature.

It was a wind tunnel. Everything was flawless. Best practices everywhere. Every row of servers was set up as hot or cold. All the heat and cold air professionally cycled through the data center. Raised floors. Doors to open and close. Well thought out.

The place smelled clean. Sterile almost.

I loved it in there. Could spend hours. Just me and the servers and that constant roar that made thinking impossible and meditation easy.

Sometimes I'd hear beeping. That meant a server was in distress. I'd have a mission then. Find the red light. Sometimes it took a while because the place was so massive. Row after row of racks. But I'd find it.

My leader and his counterpart were both kind and very organized. Wealths of knowledge who knew how to run a team.

I was eager to prove myself, to show them I could get after it with the same intensity I'd brought to my previous role. Maybe too eager.

It was day three. I was starting to feel comfortable.

I was training with a coworker who worked another shift, but I didn't want to wait for him to come in. I found some documentation in our wiki about rebuilding servers and figured I could handle it. I wanted to show them how quickly I could deliver.

Before lunch, I shut down the servers to rebuild them. The documentation said to remove the applications. I thought I was doing exactly that.

I wasn't.

What I did was delete them. From everyone. Everywhere.

The error hit at 11:47 AM.

I knew something was wrong when my pager went off.

This was a world of pagers long after pagers were common. Motorola Advisors mostly. But they were ridiculously reliable. One AA battery lasted for months. The 900MHz signal worked in basement data centers where cell phones couldn't reach. Those things could wake the dead they were so loud.

Then everyone's pager went off.

The sound started at one desk, then spread like dominoes across the floor. Beep. Beep-beep. Beep-beep-beep. A cascade of alerts that turned into a sustained electronic screaming.

People stood up from their desks. Looking around. Trying to figure out what the hell just happened.

My leader came out of his office. "Black hole event. Triage room. Now."

Black hole. That was the term for system-wide failure. The kind of event that meant all hands on deck. The kind that costs companies real money.

This healthcare system served 50,000 concurrent users across 26 states. Over 100,000 employees all over the country. Every little detail had a big impact.

It wasn't just my team. All the teams. On-calls were being rounded up into a conference room for a triage meeting. A black hole event. The whole system had gone down.

I went to the triage room and tried to help, but I was sent away. As the new guy, I didn't have what they needed. I couldn't give them context I didn't have.

I went back to my desk.

I watched people work. Looked at their screens as they checked their systems. Everyone was digging into logs, tracing connections, looking for the break point.

About 45 minutes went by. I sat there. Watching. Waiting to see if they'd figure it out.

Then a thought crept in.

Maybe it was me.

I started checking everything I'd done that day. Command history. Logs. Change records. Cross-referencing timestamps. Looking at what happened right before the black hole hit.

I went back through it again. The server rebuild. The documentation. What I thought I was doing versus what actually happened.

I was pretty sure it was me.

My stomach dropped into my shoes.

I got up. Walked to my leader's office. Maybe two minutes to the edge of the building. He had a window that looked outside. My heart was in the bottom of my throat. I was shaking.

I knocked on the door.

He was on the triage call. The door was closed. He looked up and instantly waved me in.

I walked in. Closed the door behind me.

I took a breath.

"I think I might have caused this," I said.

I explained my theory. What I'd done. When. Why I thought it triggered the black hole.

He pulled up the configuration logs. Checked. Verified.

It was me.

He unmuted the triage call. Started giving orders. Within a few minutes, they had everything restored.

"I'm prepared to walk myself out," I told him.

He looked at me. "Why would you walk yourself out?"

"I just crashed the entire system on day three."

"Your honesty is going to get you far here," he said.

I was relieved.

But I was sure the team was going to end me.

Word traveled fast in a building full of IT people. Faster than the system came back online.

By end of day, everyone knew the new guy had crashed the entire healthcare system on day three.

I walked back to my desk. My hands were still shaking.

Dan was already there, leaning against the cubicle divider. Big guy, overweight, with a heart even bigger than his frame. One of the senior engineers on the team.

He looked at me. "Why do you look... what happened? Did you figure out what broke?"

I dropped into my chair. "Yes. It was me."

"You?"

"When I went to rebuild those servers, I deleted the application from everything instead of just the servers I was rebuilding." I gestured at my monitor like the evidence was still there. *"Which caused a black hole event."*

Dan's eyebrows went up. Then he started laughing. Not mean. Just genuine surprise.

Over the next couple days, the jokes started.

Coworkers would stop by my desk. "Welcome to the team. Everybody gets one mistake. You used yours on day three."

"At least we know he can make an impact quickly."

"Still not as bad as what Tom did."

At the first team meeting after the black hole event, someone presented me with a certificate. They used Microsoft Word. Comic Sans. Some clip art. It was purposely made to look like a fourth grader did it.

"Outstanding Achievement in Not Destroying Everything."

They printed it. I kept it on my desk. It stayed there through everything. Through the financial company. Through coming back to healthcare.

It was a joke. But it was also proof I belonged.

Three weeks after the black hole event, I suggested we get drinks.

I went around the floor in person, desk to desk. "Hey, want to meet up after work? There's a place called The Library."

Whoever could make it, made it. No pressure. No formal invite.

Six of us ended up going that first night.

The Library was one of those places that tried to be clever. Bar themed like a library. The walls were lined with actual old books. They gave you a library card for their rewards program.

I thought it was hilarious.

When we walked in, it was dead. Just us and the staff. The jukebox was going. Still bright inside because it was daylight. Lots of natural light coming through the windows. The place smelled like cleaning products.

We grabbed a high top table underneath the TVs in the back corner.

Most of us ordered the same thing. A full beer, burger and fries. Simple. Cheap happy hour. Perfect.

Dan ordered a lager. I got hard cider. Strongbow. Sweet and dry. Gold colored. Popular in Ireland, so the legend says.

The conversation was easy. Life. Computer games. Technology we'd used over the years. Dan pointed at the TVs mounted in the corners.

"Look at that," he said. "Still using coax connections instead of HDMI."

I looked. "And their point of sale system is ancient."

"Nobody updates the infrastructure at restaurants," someone else said.

We weren't complaining. Just noticing. The way IT people do.

Dan and I hassled each other the whole time. That fun banter where you're testing boundaries, seeing how much you can push.

He seemed surprised I challenged him so quickly. But he pushed back as hard.

It became part of the banter. "Make sure you got your library card. We got to go study after work."

The Library became our place. Sometimes five of us. Sometimes eight. But there were regulars.

People from all kinds of roles. Networking. Servers. All different levels. A melting pot. There were no titles at the bar.

Dan was one of them.

It was a Thursday in April when he told me.

We were at The Library. Four of us that night. Around 5 PM, right after work. Still light out. Sitting at a high top table with the fake bookshelves behind us.

I had my Strongbow. Dan had his lager.

Dan had a deep voice. Always wore a polo shirt and dress pants. Comfortable but still professional. The way he sat when he was processing a problem was almost like something out of a movie.

We were talking about the usual stuff. Work. Weekend plans.

Then Dan gestured at his stomach. His whole torso, really. The weight he'd been carrying for years.

"Look at this," he said. His face was hopeful. Determined. "I'm done with how it became this. I'm going to change all of it."

I leaned forward. "Yeah?"

"Yeah," he said. He seemed animated. Alive. "I've been planning it. I'm gonna make it happen."

"When?" I asked.

"Soon," he said. "I just want to wait for the right moment."

I took a drink. "Don't wait too long. Perfect doesn't exist."

He laughed. Raised his glass. "I know. I want to make sure it's right."

We clinked glasses. Drank to his future.

We kept talking. About life. About dreams. About doing things now. About how many people I'd met who died with their dreams still in them.

Dan had one of the biggest hearts I'd ever encountered. He cared so much about people. Would remember your birthday. Would ask how your weekend was and actually listen.

He was planning to change his life. Change everything.

I believed in him.

Little did we know perfect doesn't exist.

They brought me on full-time in June 2012.

The same day I signed the lease on my one-bedroom apartment.

The same day the sheriff's sale notice appeared on the side door of my house, by where I parked. I was halfway through the thirty days they'd given me to clean it out and leave.

It was also the anniversary of my bike accident.

It's one of those days.

Life at healthcare settled into a rhythm I wasn't used to. Work stayed at work. I had time for things outside the office.

The Library nights continued. Dan was still one of the regulars.

Then I moved to the financial company. Different building. Different team. But we stayed in touch.

Dan went home after his collapse. Worked remotely. We didn't do video calls. Just phone calls. All of us would call sometimes, to check in and see how he was doing.

His breathing had something labored about it. A little more wheezing than before.

He worked from home for the next two months. Limited movement. Fighting.

His breathing would get weird on conference calls. That labored quality. The wheezing. You could hear it through the speaker.

He'd just bought a house. He'd driven me by it once, so proud. Showed me the yard, the garage, everything he was planning to do with it.

He never got to spend a single night there.

He died the day before Thanksgiving.

I was driving to my parents' house for Thanksgiving dinner. The expressway was busy but moving. Just before the rest area between my place and theirs. My truck was a 5-speed manual.

My phone rang.

My old leader. From the healthcare job.

I answered.

"Hate to call you on a holiday, but I just found out Dan passed away and wanted to let you know."

I pulled into the rest area. Put the truck in neutral. Set the parking brake.

I sat there for a few minutes.

Then I got back on the expressway and drove to my parents' house.

My mom saw it on my face the moment I walked in. She didn't ask questions. Pulled me into a hug.

3-4:
THE HELPER
(2012-2020)

My time with CERT (Community Emergency Response Team) started in 2012. I'd stay with them in two cities until 2016, learning basic disaster response skills. Our uniform was practical: polo shirt, reflective vest, walkie talkie, first aid kit, and Go Bags filled with tools to shut off gas lines and handle natural disasters. Heavy-duty tactical backpacks kept in the vehicle. Inside: a four-way sillcock key for shutting off water, a gas shut-off wrench, high-visibility marking tape, and trauma shears.

My most meaningful day was at a local art fair, partnered with a Middle Eastern woman wearing a hijab. The sun was out, the mood was light. We walked between booths talking about our favorite places in town.

That's when we saw her: a little girl, all by herself, completely mesmerized by a bubble machine. Hundreds of iridescent spheres floating in the sunlight. In the center of the chaotic crowd, they created a silent zone where she stood perfectly still, eyes wide, completely detached from the frantic movement around her. We'd seen her earlier with her parents. In that instant, without saying a word, we both knew what to do.

No panic. No dramatic rushing. My partner walked over and started talking to the little girl in a soothing voice, becoming an anchor of safety in the middle of the crowded fair. At the same time, I got on the radio with our location and a description.

For four minutes we were in heightened awareness, scanning the crowd for frantic parents while keeping the girl safe and calm.

Finally, we saw them: a crying mother and a father whose face was pure terror. The relief when they spotted their daughter was immediate and overwhelming. A police officer came over and gave the little girl a sticker badge, instantly turning any fear into excitement and pride.

A year later, in 2017, I moved to a new city. My old instinct kicked in: find a way to get involved. This city didn't have a CERT team, so I had two options: Police Auxiliary or the Animal Shelter. I applied for both the same day. I was already months into training with the police before the animal shelter even got back to me.

The Police Auxiliary was an education in reading people and situations. Every shift began with a ritual: pressing my uniform, making sure everything was clean and correct. Baby blue polyester-blend shirt with permanent military-grade creases. Every piece of metal polished with a microfiber cloth to remove fingerprints. The heavy Kevlar vest went on underneath. A stiff, hot hug that never let up. The panels were thick enough to blunt my range of motion, forcing me to sit perfectly upright. It trapped every bit of body heat, creating a micro-climate of sweat against my skin that stayed there for the entire four-hour shift.

This wasn't about vanity. When I put on that uniform, I wasn't Tom anymore. I was representing the community.

Taking the vest off at the end of the night was a physical transformation. When you pull those Velcro straps apart and lift the weight off your shoulders, the rush of cool air hitting your damp undershirt is a religious experience. You finally understand the collective sigh of relief people describe when they take off a restrictive bra at the end of a long day.

During training, they told us a story, probably more myth than reality in the law enforcement world, but they tell it because it drives home a point. Two officers responded to accidents at the same spot within a week. First officer: crisp uniform, excellent shape. The driver took the ticket and left. Second officer: sloppy uniform, out of shape. The same driver killed him.

It's an extreme story. But walking into a room in a crisp uniform with a Kevlar vest changes how people respond to you.

Most shifts, maybe 99% of the time, were quiet. School zone patrols, checking business doors after hours, sitting behind broken-down cars on busy roads. Park patrols, home checks for people out of town. Routine stuff that we did to assist the regular officers.

One night we got called to an apartment building fire alarm. The firefighters determined it was a burned-out relay: no actual fire. Residents were cleared to go back inside.

What happened next was pure spontaneous joy. Everyone had brought their dogs out during the evacuation, and in the grassy area in front of the building, all the dogs started playing together. A golden retriever wrestling with a bulldog, tails wagging in a blur. Different breeds, different sizes, different personalities, all suddenly free to interact without human anxiety getting in the way. The sharp mechanical beep-beep-beep of the fire alarm gave way to a dozen dogs talking in the grass.

I spent twenty minutes petting dogs and watching neighbors who'd probably never spoken before laughing and chatting like old friends.

Some nights were anything but routine.

Months later, we were on patrol one evening when a BOLO came over the radio. "Be on Lookout" for a man in distress. The dispatcher's tone was clipped and fast—high priority. My partner and I were already at a school near the location and started scanning the area, looking for anything unusual.

A few minutes later, a pedestrian flagged us down and pointed toward the bushes next to a school. "There's a guy hiding in there."

We pulled over. I got out and approached carefully, my partner hanging back as backup. The man emerged from the bushes with hunched shoulders and clenched fists. His eyes were darting and unfocused, looking for a target to vent his pressure. Every word, every gesture was designed to escalate.

My training said to use standard de-escalation techniques: speak calmly, create distance, don't match his energy. But watching him work himself up, standard wasn't going to cut it. I needed to short-circuit his pattern entirely.

"What's your favorite omelet?" I asked, voice even and calm.

He stopped mid-rant. His jaw went slack. "What?"

I keyed my radio while he was still processing, giving dispatch our location.

"Are you a griddle guy?" I continued, rattling off breakfast foods as fast as I could. "Pancakes? Blueberry, strawberry, chocolate chip? French toast?"

His posture deflated. His shoulders dropped. The red alert energy vanished, replaced by a dull, safe confusion.

He went from aggressive to confused, which was all I needed. No longer a threat to anyone, including himself. By the time backup arrived maybe a minute later, he was calm enough for them to get help without anyone getting hurt.

Then a year later, the jumper call. The tension was palpable when we arrived. We were the second car. Our job was closing the road, re-routing traffic and onlookers from becoming part of the crisis.

I looked over. A stranger had pulled over and bear-hugged the individual. No protocol, no procedure. Just one human holding another.

As quickly as it started, the situation was resolved. We packed up and went back to patrol, driving through downtown where people were eating outside and laughing, completely unaware of the tragedy that had been averted.

I left the Police Auxiliary in January 2020 to become a motivational speaker. I gave one speech.

Then the pandemic locked everything down.

3-5:
DOWNTOWN
(2013-2014)

The recruiter called in late summer 2013.

"I've got a Windows infrastructure position at a financial company downtown. Contract work. The money is significantly more than what you're making now."

He told me the number.

It was significantly more.

I'd been at the healthcare company for almost two years. Crashed their system on day three. Got the certificate a year later for not destroying everything again. Spent Thursday nights at The Library with Dan and the crew. Good work. Stable. But when someone offers you that much more money, you listen.

I took the job.

Left healthcare in September 2013.

The building was circular. Twenty-three floors of glass and steel downtown. No corners anywhere. The cubicles wrapped around in gentle curves following the shape of the floor.

I sat in one of eight cubes arranged around a small table in the middle of our section. From my desk I could see out across the entire floor. Watch people moving through the space. See all the way to the windows on the other side.

The team was mostly contractors. Eighty percent of us. Brought in to fix specific problems. Big guys. All of them. Smart as hell. The kind of people who could talk about anything and make it interesting.

I was the smallest one there. At five eleven I'm not short. But every single one of them had at least a few inches on me. The scrappy one surrounded by giants. I'd always been comfortable with that dynamic.

This was also when I was getting into roller derby. I started bringing my GoPro cameras with me every day. Recording videos. I never knew what I was going to experience.

On practice nights I'd carpool with a derby skater who worked nearby. We'd leave downtown together. Head to the track.

My job was what I always did. Fix problems. Computer issues. Things not working right. The usual technical fires that need putting out.

I was good at it. I've always been good at walking into broken systems and figuring out what's wrong.

The work itself was fine. Interesting enough at first. But that wasn't what mattered.

Springtime in Detroit is an adventure. The weather shifts constantly. Rain storms that flood the expressways one hour.

Sudden bursts of sun that make the glass buildings gleam the next. Wind that whips between skyscrapers and catches you off guard when you turn a corner.

I loved it. The aesthetic of it. The way the city felt alive and unpredictable.

But it was the lunches that changed everything.

The team went out almost every day. Not fancy corporate lunches with clients or presentations. Just walking somewhere. Finding food. Exploring. Talking. We'd walk blocks sometimes. Pick a direction and see what we'd find.

That's when I started learning downtown like a local instead of a visitor.

There was a German bar we'd go to. Jacoby's. Been there since 1904. Tucked down Brush Street. Inside it's dark wood, low ceilings. The smell hit you the moment you walked in. Red cabbage and fried potatoes. Schnitzel and sauerbraten. Boot of beer and potato pancakes. The kind of place that felt like an escape from the glass towers.

The staff knew their regulars. People would talk to you if you let them. Ask questions. Share stories. I'd sit there listening to people who'd lived in Detroit their whole lives tell me about what the city used to be. What it was becoming. What they hoped it would be. Stories I'd never heard in years of living in the suburbs.

One of the guys at the bar worked in economics. We'd talk about finding good food on a budget. He knew every place downtown where you could get a solid lunch for under fifteen bucks. Not fast food. Real food. Places with history. Places that cared.

I took notes. Started building my own map of the city.

I found two brunch places. Hudson Cafe on Woodward. During the week I could get in, but weekends it was a 2 hour wait. The line always wraps around the corner. I'd get Voodoo Red Velvet pancakes or Cinnabun crepes. So good I kept going back.

The Dime Store tucked inside an old building. They had this Boar Sausage Benny that I loved. Duck Billed platters. Good food in a place that felt right. Started researching BBQ joints. That became its own thing. A whole side quest. Keeping notes on different places. Planning return visits. Comparing styles. Figuring out what I liked and why.

Sometimes we'd get one person to walk to their car while the rest of us ran to Potato Palace or Slows BBQ. Potato Palace near Wayne State. They'd load up a baked potato the size of a football. Heavy, warm meal that reset your brain. Slows in Corktown. The Yardbird sandwich. Smoked chicken with mushrooms and bacon. Worth the sprint.

There was a Mexican restaurant we'd go to regularly. Loco's. In Greektown even though it was Mexican. Massive margaritas. Trash can nachos. Loud and fun.

Got to know the staff by name. They knew us. We'd walk in and they'd already know what we usually ordered. So many good meals there. The kind of place where you felt like family.

I found the alleys. Not sketchy back alleys. Photogenic pedestrian alleys with murals painted on the walls. Contemporary art galleries. Bars. Restaurants. A music club. The kind of spaces that felt alive. The kind even people from the suburbs wouldn't be afraid to walk through. Shortcuts that saved you blocks of walking in winter.

I found dive bars that served cheap lunch. Some were just cheap. But some were unique. Good food. Interesting people. The kind of places you'd never find unless someone told you about them.

I talked to strangers everywhere. Asked questions. Where's the best coffee? Where do you go when you want quiet? What's changed in the last five years?

One was trained in martial arts. He told me at every corner do a quick three sixty look. Make sure you're aware of your surroundings. Not paranoid. Just aware. Know what's happening around you.

Another gave me different advice. "If someone acts crazy and makes you uncomfortable, be more crazy than them. They'll leave you alone."

One of the guys had his wallet taken. A block later the cops stopped the person. Asked them to give the wallet back. Got it. Handed it to my coworker. Then said the best they could do was drive the guy who mugged him across town and drop him off.

Detroit doesn't have much jail space. You have to do something pretty bad to actually go to jail.

These were people who knew how to live in the city. How to navigate it. How to stay safe without being scared.

I tested the advice sooner than expected.

I was leaving Hudson Cafe after work one evening. A man approached me on the sidewalk, talking nonsense. Loud. Agitated. Getting closer.

He started walking toward me.

I put my hand inside my coat. Slowly. Like I was resting it on something. I looked him dead in the eyes and gave him the craziest look I could manage.

He stopped in his tracks.

He followed me for a few blocks. Keeping distance but not leaving. I kept walking. Didn't speed up. Didn't look back more than once.

Then I turned around and told him he was my friend and I wanted to buy him food.

He got so confused he disappeared from my view.

I kept walking. Heart pounding. But walking.

We'd walk to the parking garage together at night. At least in pairs. For safety.

One of my coworkers lived in Canada. When his dad passed away I gathered donations from the team and went to the funeral. We were close-knit like that.

There were so many coffee options downtown. One place on Woodward had clear tubes running across the ceiling. You'd order and watch the beans zip through the tubes. Drop into the roaster right in front of you. Fresh as you could get. I found coffee there that actually gave me energy instead of just calming me down. It was fine. I was walking a lot while working downtown.

I started going up to the higher floors of the building when I had time. Twenty-third floor was ours. But some of the meeting rooms were higher. You could see the whole city from up there. The river. Belle Isle. The buildings spreading out in all directions.

The higher you got, the more you could see.

We'd go to Coach Insignia for happy hour. Seventy-first floor. You'd take this glass elevator that shot up the side of the tower. Your ears would pop. The city would unfold beneath you.

After work we'd get drinks and stare at the water. Windsor across the river. Seventy-one floors up.

I'd take the People Mover sometimes. That elevated train that loops around downtown. Gliding between skyscrapers.

One day I was getting on the People Mover to go to lunch and heard an explosion. The kind where people actually made it their business to know what it was. Turns out it was Autorama. They had a road closed off for semi truck drag racing. Detroit being Detroit.

Winter that year was brutal.

I loved working downtown. Loved the building. Loved the city. But the commute in winter was something else. Ice storms all winter long. The kind where you'd leave for work at six in the morning and wouldn't get there until nine because the roads were sheets of ice. Or you'd leave at five and still be crawling home at eight. Everyone moving at fifteen miles per hour. White knuckling the wheel. Watching for ice.

I didn't care.

That's the weird part. I should have hated it. Most people did. But I loved it. The adventure of it. The challenge. The fact that I was going somewhere worth going to. I'd sit in traffic watching the snow fall and think about where I'd go for lunch the next day.

Campus Martius had an ice skating rink in winter. Real sand and lounge chairs in summer. Right in the middle of downtown.

I'd walk. Explore. Get lost on purpose and find my way back.

One day at lunch I stumbled into a place that looked like it had been there forever. Figured I'd give it a try. The place was busy. Staff came over and said they were closed. I looked around. Everyone was in suits. Almost like a mob movie. Who knows. I got out of there quickly. Laughed when I got outside.

One of my favorites was cutting through the Guardian Building. Wasn't faster. Wasn't a shortcut. But I loved walking through it. Orange brick on the outside. Inside was all these colors. Blues and golds. The ceiling looked hand-painted. The whole place glowed. Like someone decided a bank should be beautiful instead of boring.

I'd grab coffee and sit in the lobby sometimes. Just looking around. They built it in 1929. You could tell people cared when they built it. Made things that lasted.

I got to see the people who really lived downtown. Meet them. Talk to them.

I wasn't just working downtown anymore. I was part of it.

Then came Youmacon.

November 2013. Thursday afternoon. Around three. I was coming back from lunch and started seeing the hotel fill up with characters. Anime characters. Video game characters. Costumes everywhere. People in full makeup and wigs and props that must have taken months to make.

I'd never watched anime. Didn't know anything about it. But I couldn't stop staring.

The bosses came by. "Youmacon's starting. This building is going to be chaos. You can head out early if you want."

I grabbed my things. Started to leave. Then I saw a Pikachu walking by. Right past our Windows Infrastructure team. Yellow fur, red cheeks, lightning bolt tail. Followed it. Started talking to people. Making friends. Before I knew it I was in it for the weekend.

I didn't go home.

I just wandered. Watched. People watching. Everyone was so friendly. Happy to talk about their costumes. About the characters they were dressed as. About why they loved this convention. About their passions.

I joked that my costume was corporate IT guy. I was literally dressed for work. Button-down shirt. Slacks. The whole thing. People thought it was hilarious.

I hung out until late that night. Came back the next day. And the day after that. Learning about a whole world I'd never known existed.

I came back the next few years. Got to break out my crazy suits. The loud ones. The ones that made people smile.

The building made it easy. The elevator banks went off in a circle into different towers. One tower in the middle was a hotel with a convention center attached. We worked in one of the side towers. You could just walk right over.

The work itself was a different story.

When I work a job I go in hard. Find every issue. Untangle every mess. Get systems running smoothly. Make things better than they were. It's satisfying. That feeling when something that was broken starts working. When problems disappear. When everything runs the way it's supposed to.

But once the problems are solved something shifts.

I stop looking for them. Not because I don't care. But because they're not there anymore. I've fixed them. The systems work. Everything runs. And when there's nothing left to fix I don't know what to do with myself.

By October 2014 I'd been there thirteen months. The infrastructure issues I came to fix were fixed. Everything ran smoothly. The team was great. The work was stable.

But I was restless.

I sat at my desk. Everything running smoothly. No fires to put out. Nothing broken. I stared out the curved windows at the city.

I couldn't sit still anymore.

3-6:
THE FARM
(2013-2014)

Two months after losing the house, I was trying to figure out what life looked like when you weren't working all the time.

The healthcare job was stable. Solid hours, work that stayed at work. After years of the law firm's brutal schedule, having actual free time felt strange. I didn't know what to do with myself.

So I started exploring. I'd load a 35mm camera with black and white film and drive the back roads around Michigan. Old barns, abandoned buildings, landscapes that caught the light in interesting ways.

I needed to create a new life. I didn't know what that looked like yet.

That's how I found the tack sale. I didn't know what "tack" was. I was driving, saw a sign, followed it to a farm. People were browsing saddles and bridles and equipment I couldn't identify. I walked around taking pictures.

I hated horses.

Not feared them. Not felt uncomfortable around them. Hated them.

I had no reason to. Everyone else seemed to love them. But something about horses made my skin crawl, made me want to keep my distance, made me irrationally angry in a way I couldn't explain.

Within months I was volunteering.

Parades became my life for the next two years. I'd run along the routes with Nick, my right-hand man, scanning for kids who might dart too close to the horses. Safety first. Horses, riders, people watching. In that order. But also having fun. Figuring it out as we went.

One parade stands out. A holiday night parade, everything glowing with lights. It was cold, snowing, everything you'd expect for a parade but at night. I'd set up my tripod for the low light, ready to capture the moment.

The sheriff's horses were near us. Something spooked them.

You felt it first. A shudder going up from the horses, then a high-pitched squeal as they reared up on their back legs. The sheriff was instantly able to bring them back down to calm, professional and quick. But whatever had spooked that horse had zero impact on ours.

Our horses stood there. Totally unbothered.

I moved quickly and quietly toward our team. The horses recognized me by then. They were as unphased by me as they were by everything else happening around them. The smell of burning wood drifted over from fire pits on nearby patios as we passed.

Our horses had no point of view about anything. They'd been desensitized to havoc. Prepared through controlled exposure to the unpredictable. Hanging pool noodles, blowing grocery bags, blaring sirens, remote control cars. They'd seen it all.

My cousin recommended a book: Zen Horse, Zen Mind by Allan J. Hamilton. A neurosurgeon who was also a horseman. I started reading it at home, then at my cousin's house, borrowing his copy until I got my own.

The book talked about a horse nobody could control and a kid in a wheelchair who loved that horse. They were best friends. They understood each other. The kid was disabled, had special needs, and was the only one who could calm this particular horse.

Horses don't respond to what you're saying or what you're trying to project. They respond to what you are in that moment. They're prey animals. They scan your heart rate, your muscle tension. If you show up with work brain, high energy, fast pulse, they read predator. They have no room for bullshit. They see right through it all.

I started taking pictures around the farm when I'd visit. Then they put me to work in the barn. Lift the hay bales, one after another, feeling for any that felt extra heavy. If they did, cut them open. They'd be hot. Chemical reaction from bacteria when hay is baled with too much moisture. Hot enough to burn your hand, like touching a radiator. That meant they got wet and started to decompose. This is how barn fires started.

Then I was given keys to a golf cart with a barrel to collect road apples from the field. Horse manure. Grassy, earthy smell.

Nothing like the sterile hospital scent from my day job. I'd drive around with the rake, collect them, head back to drop them off.

One of the little girls, Piper, maybe ten years old, asked if I was gonna ride.

I said no way. I don't like horses. I like farms.

She laughed. "Your horse will be ready after you dump the barrel."

Piper put me on a horse without asking permission.

Her first lesson was stupidly simple: "Heels down, look where you want to go." That was it. She led me around the arena on a lead rope while I tried to remember which way was heels down.

I was scared and excited.

Word got out that the weird camera guy was riding. Other riders started teaching me things. Before I knew it, I had half a dozen instructors, each one adding their own advice.

Horses were big, organic, and unpredictable. Not like technology that gives consistent results. That's why I hated them. They weren't predictable.

My dad had dug out a photo when he found out I was doing the horse farm. Me as a baby, under two years old, sitting on a horse with the biggest smile on my face. I was amused.

All my worries vanished. The only thing that mattered was being on that horse. It was like we became one.

If I didn't get my inner game calm, they wouldn't let me ride them. Simple as that.

I slowed down after work. Speeches on my drive in, music on the way home. A playlist for the drive to the farm. When I heard those songs, my body would start to relax before I even pulled into the driveway.

I started wearing my cowboy boots everywhere with my jeans and big belt buckle. Square-toe ropers. The weight of the boot, the height of the heel. Changed how I walked. At first, I thought it was for fun.

Then I had a date. I figured I'd dress normal. Dress pants, dress shirt, dress shoes. We were meeting at a bar in a little downtown area.

We said hi, ordered our drinks. For about an hour, we talked. All of it about her. Her favorite TV shows, the characters she enjoyed. I asked if she had any hobbies.

"All I do is work," she said.

I wanted to ask why she was even dating, but I didn't. She didn't ask much about me. Then she told me I must be boring.

I let it die there. I had no interest in getting to know this woman anymore. She'd told me everything I needed to know.

When I put my boots back on, I didn't care anymore about the date that bombed.

The boots and jeans weren't the costume. The dress pants were the costume.

3-7:
THE MASTER KEY
(2012-PRESENT)

I found float tanks the way most people find things that save them. By accident. Someone mentioned them. I didn't think much of it until I did.

This was around 2012. I was working at the healthcare system, after the law firm. The nearest float tank was 90 minutes away at someone's house. An actual house. You'd ring the doorbell, they'd let you into their basement, and there were two tanks. One was coffin style, the other was a clamshell that closed around you like a Polly Pocket.

I drove those three hours round trip because something about the description made sense. Total sensory deprivation. No sound. No light. Nothing but you and your thoughts in water so full of Epsom salt that you float like a cork.

The first session was strange. The pod was like a coffin with a hinge. You'd climb in, pull the door shut, and your brain would have to adjust. But after ten minutes, something shifted. The water was exactly body temperature. 93.5 degrees. Skin-receptor neutral. After a while, you couldn't tell where your skin ended and the water began.

My brain finally shut up.

Not forever. Just for an hour. But that hour felt like two weeks off the grid somewhere tropical. A vacation I didn't know I needed.

I kept going. Different places as they opened. An insurance office basement. Various centers around the area. I'd often go after reading a self-help book, using the tank to digest what I'd read, to let the ideas sink in without the usual mental chatter. Floating became so much a part of my life that I don't remember what life was like without it.

I started doing experiments on my body. Took a month where I only listened to music without words in it. Testing things. Seeing what stuck.

I'd go once a week. Sometimes twice if I was working through something heavy. But driving 90 minutes each way was a commitment. The technology evolved over time too. The early places, you had to call or email to book. No online scheduling.

Then one day I was driving home and saw it. A sign for Motor City Float. Right there. Ten minutes from my house instead of 90.

I pulled in to check it out.

Too good to be true. Closer. Lower cost. Better equipment. And the staff were people I actually wanted to talk to.

June 21, 2017. 11am. Room 3.

My first float at Motor City Float.

I remember the exact time because it felt like crossing a threshold. Everything before had been practice. This was where it all clicked.

The first time I called to book, my caller ID still showed "Tom Awesome." I'd changed it years ago as a joke when I was younger, back when you could customize what showed up on people's phones. I'd forgotten it was still set that way.

The staff thought it was hilarious. The name stuck. They've called me Tom Awesome ever since.

They even set up a promo code AWESOME for me to refer people. I laughed so hard the first time I saw it logging into my portal.

Motor City Float wasn't like the basement pods or the house tanks. This was built from the ground up for the experience.

The tanks weren't pods. They were float cabins. Walk-in suites with high ceilings. Seven feet tall. You could stand up fully inside before lying down. The water surface was the size of a queen bed. You could spread your arms and legs wide without touching the walls.

Each cabin held around 1,000 pounds of medical-grade Epsom salt dissolved in ten inches of water. The solution was so dense you floated effortlessly. No effort. No adjustment. Just instant weightlessness.

The ceiling was embedded with hundreds of tiny fiber-optic lights. A starry night sky. It made the space feel infinite instead of enclosed. You had control over everything. LED colors cycling through the spectrum. Deep blue. Soft red. Or you could shut it all off and go pitch black.

The audio system used underwater transducers. High-end speakers that vibrated through the water instead of the air. When music played, you didn't just hear it. You felt it through your skeleton. Ambient tracks. Guided meditations. Or silence.

Once the lights went off and the music faded, there was nothing. No input. No stimulation. Just you and the absence of everything else.

It was the exact opposite of everything I'd ever known at work. Just silence.

The first time I went full sensory deprivation at Motor City Float, I understood why people called it a master key.

The door closed. The lights faded. The music dissolved into nothing.

For the first few minutes, my brain fought it. Kept generating noise. Running through tomorrow's meetings. Replaying conversations. The usual loop. I could feel my jaw clenching. My shoulders were up near my ears even though there was nothing to brace against.

Then my breathing slowed. My heartbeat became the loudest thing in the room. I could hear blood moving through my ears. A low, rhythmic swoosh.

The water erased my edges. I couldn't feel my arms. Couldn't tell if my eyes were open or closed. My body dissolved into the warm dark and I was floating in nothing. No up. No down. No walls. No ceiling. No skin.

Thoughts kept surfacing. But instead of spiraling, they'd rise, sit there, and dissolve. Like watching clouds from underneath. Problems I'd been grinding on for weeks would appear with a clarity I couldn't access at my desk. Solutions I'd missed because I was too busy running to see them.

When the music came back on — the gentle signal that the session was ending — I had no idea if it had been thirty minutes or three hours.

I stood up. The salt water ran off me in sheets. My muscles felt like they'd been unplugged from the grid. My face was slack. My jaw was open. I caught my reflection in the shower glass and didn't recognize the expression. It was calm. Genuinely calm. I couldn't remember the last time my face had looked like that.

An hour in the tank felt like hitting a reset button I didn't know existed.

The staff became friends. Real friends. People I'd see outside the float center. People who understood why someone would drive across town to lie in salt water for an hour in complete darkness.

That's how I met Jade. She worked the front desk but also did Reiki. We'd talk after sessions. Eventually, those conversations became something more.

Jade mentioned she did Reiki. I had no idea what that meant, but I said yes anyway.

During the session, Jade moved around me like a little fairy.

The treatment room was quiet. Still air that smelled of palo santo.

I lay on the massage table under a weighted blanket. The glass beads inside shifted with a soft sound. My nervous system got the message: threat assessment off.

Then I felt it. A dry, radiating warmth held an inch above my skin. My muscles started to uncoil. The tension in my jaw and behind my eyes began to dissolve.

Behind my eyelids, pulses of color moved. An internal light show replacing the server rack status lights.

For a moment, I lost the map of my body. Couldn't tell where my arms ended and the table began.

I stepped off the table feeling lighter.

The center had other services. Cold plunge. Sauna. Red light therapy. A tea room designed to ease you back into the world before you walked out and returned to the noise.

The sauna was in my blood. The cold plunge sucked. My life hack was bringing an attractive friend.

But the float tank was the core. The thing that made everything else work.

That's when I started going more often. Once a week. Sometimes five times if I was working through something heavy.

I used every service they offered over the years. Became a regular. Then became part of the community they built. The kind of place where people weren't just customers. They were people working on themselves. People who needed the quiet.

The float center owners all knew each other too. They were happy I'd found a place that worked for me with ease.

Floating became routine maintenance. Like clearing cache. Like defragging a hard drive. When my brain started running too many background processes, I'd float. When I came out, everything was indexed properly again.

Some sessions, I'd have massive realizations. Breakthroughs that changed how I saw something I'd been stuck on for months. Other sessions, nothing happened. I'd just float. Rest. Let my nervous system remember what it felt like to not be on high alert.

The tanks didn't fix everything. But they gave me space to process what needed processing. A place where my body was finally allowed to be off call.

Twenty years of being the person who fixed things. The person who responded when systems failed. The person who stayed late, came in early, carried the pager, monitored the alerts.

In the float tank, none of that existed. No alerts. No emergencies. No one needing anything from me.

Just salt water. Darkness. Silence.

And for the first time in a long time, that was enough.

3-8:
DERBY CHURCH
(2014-2016)

The inspiration wasn't the movie Whip It, though everyone always assumed it was. My catalyst was watching Hannah transform.

Before derby, Hannah was quiet and tiny like a mouse. She was there, but you had to be actively looking for her to see her.

After a few months on skates, she was leading conversations. She looked comfortable in her body. She didn't give two shits what anyone thought about her. She was there to have fun.

I needed to find out what was happening in that warehouse.

But I had a problem. I was physically weak.

The boot camp for new skaters was called "Fresh Meat." The slogan was an old Japanese proverb: "Fall down seven times, get up eight."

It took me three full waves to master the basic skills. Wave 8, "The Crazy 8's." Wave 9. Finally passing with Wave 10.

The practice space was a barely heated warehouse called "The Mint." An ironic joke based on Thin Mint cookies because we were all frozen. Maybe 60 degrees in the winter. Crisp enough you could see your breath until the pack heated up the room. Great when you were practicing. We all had zip-up hoodies we wore everywhere.

We learned to skate on unforgiving concrete. The sound was echo-y, every movement amplified. Later, when I visited the men's league on their wooden rink, the difference was striking. The wood absorbed so much of the sound.

The drills were surprisingly fun. Learning to fall safely, stop quickly, jump over cones.

During one practice, we were doing pack drills. Staying in a pack, going in circles over and over again, weaving in and out. Before I knew it, I messed up. Twisted my ankle. I went down.

I heard the whistles blow. Everything stopped. Everyone took a knee.

I knew it was for me.

I was angry.

I was done. I had a cane for a bit after that and did NSO duties. Non-skating official. Penalty box timer. Watching from the sidelines while my body healed.

It took me until the second bootcamp to get my 25 laps in 5 minutes.

One of my friends, a skater on the A team, was counting my laps before they started their practice. When they told me I got it, I was excited. They were rough and tough looking, but I knew the truth. They were one of the kindest people you would ever meet.

The smell in summer was unforgettable. Sweat, determination, industrial cleaner. Restaurants would seat us away from other diners after practice. None of us realized how bad we reeked until we were back in the civilian world.

But the real church happened after practice.

On Sundays, we'd all go to the diner at the end of the road. On weeknights, we'd hit other local spots. I developed a simple method for organizing these gatherings. Instead of convincing people to come, I'd make an open invitation. "A bunch of us are going to eat, come join us."

The most memorable ritual was the whiskey slap after bouts.

We'd pile into a local bar, still sweaty and bruised, riding the high of exhaustion and team solidarity. We'd circle up, everyone holding a shot of whiskey in one hand, the other ready to slap. When it started, we went around the circle. Slap, shoot, slap, shoot.

Some could use their full body weight, knew how to give a hearty full-face slap. The kind you prayed for because it distributed the energy across a larger surface area. A palm slap thuds. A fingertip slap stings. You wanted the thud. Others like me would stand there laughing at the absurdity, enjoying every round until someone who did CrossFit or worked manual labor finally took me down.

It often became a test of endurance, continuing until only a few people were left standing. I'd frequently make it to the final rounds, doing my best not to react to the sting. The most they ever got from me was a watery eye and then laughter.

The bartenders loved us. We were entertainment and reliably sold out their whiskey supply within an hour. I was grateful it was within walking distance of my apartment. Not because of the alcohol, but because your equilibrium was shot from having your head snapped around by people who spent their free time bodychecking each other.

I would totally do it again.

When I finally passed my skills test after three waves of Fresh Meat, I had a choice to make. Leave my league and join a men's team or stay and train to become a referee.

For weeks, I couldn't decide. Mike, "Ecto-1" as we called him in derby, and I visited the men's league. We warmed up at an open skate before their practice. The space was a wooden rink with all the lights and music, a completely different vibe from our concrete warehouse.

That's when it happened.

A kid fell right in front of me on the track. Without thinking, all my derby skills kicked in. I jumped clean over the child, stopped on a dime, and skated back to check on them. The kid was fine, more impressed than hurt, thinking what I'd done was the coolest thing they'd ever seen.

The vibe at the men's league wasn't quite right, and it was a long drive from everything I knew. Deep down, I wasn't ready to leave my home league family.

My salvation came during those Sunday carpools to practice. Four of us cramped into a car together, three other skaters and me, driving that small stretch of farmland between the rink and where we all lived.

The Fresh Meat bootcamp had been intense for all of us. Lots of personal stuff came up during those conversations. Relationship struggles, work stress, family drama, the way derby was changing how we saw ourselves in the world.

When I kept fishing for answers about my derby decision, one of them finally said it.

"Stop trying to get us to decide for you. It's your life. You get to choose."

My mind was blown.

I didn't want to leave my league family for a men's team that felt like foreign territory. I wanted to stay with my people. Becoming a referee was the path that would keep me connected to this world.

Referee practice was multiple nights a week and most weekends. I was often the backup referee, the one who'd get to go out if anyone got hurt. Mostly, I watched, soaking it all in.

But first, I had to learn the Fox40 whistle.

I didn't know it was like playing an instrument. I thought you blew it. Four separate blows, right? Wrong. It's one blow and four tongue flicks. The Fox40 has no moving parts, no pea to jam. You need diaphragmatic breath and tongue-blocking to create the staccato tweet-tweet-tweet-tweet of a lead jammer call-off.

I practiced outdoors because it's a loud whistle. Over and over until I finally got it right.

Derby requires six referees on the track. Two tracking the jammers, one managing the pack, and three on the outside.

My favorite position was outside ref. You got to move in two directions, go fast, stop fast, pivot on a dime. You traveled a larger circumference than the inside refs. Had to master the crossover to keep up with the jammers. High-speed lateral stride like a speed skater's gait. The inside refs had less space to work with, boxed in by the pack.

Watching the refs work was fascinating. Being part of it, even as backup, was something else entirely. You had to read the entire track at once, anticipate where the chaos would erupt, position yourself to see what needed to be seen. It was like solving a puzzle in real time while skating backwards.

3-9:
THE MAKER
(2014-2019)

I've always been someone who creates things with my hands. The giant cupcake car drove past me, and I started laughing.

Someone had looked at the world and thought, 'You know what this needs? A drivable Hostess cupcake.' And then they built it.

That was Maker Faire in a nutshell, a spirit of joyful invention I found year after year at The Henry Ford Museum of American Innovation in Dearborn, Michigan. For years, I'd make the trip to volunteer at Maker Faire Detroit, a two-day festival that brought together everyone from inventors and robotics enthusiasts to urban farmers and traditional craftspeople, all united by a single belief: if you can imagine it, you can make it.

I would spend the entire weekend volunteering there, helping people navigate the sprawling grounds and find the exhibits and workshops that matched their curiosity. During orientation, we were told something that became a kind of philosophy: you never tell someone no. If you don't know the answer, you always tell them you'll get it for them. I did back-to-back shifts giving people directions, constantly moving through the space, watching people's faces light up when they found exactly what they were looking for.

The Henry Ford complex itself is a testament to American ingenuity and innovation, housing everything from Abraham Lincoln's chair from Ford's Theatre to Rosa Parks' bus to JFK's presidential limousine. During Maker Faire, this already incredible space transformed into something even more surreal and wonderful.

Walking the grounds was like stepping into a fever dream of creativity. I'd round a corner and find high schoolers explaining how their robot navigated obstacle courses. The robotics demonstrations were incredible: kids who couldn't even drive yet were programming machines to make complex decisions.

I'd move on and find some of my favorite aerial instructors performing improvised routines. They were demonstrating skills on silks and lyra that looked effortless but I knew were incredibly difficult. They were in performance mode with a crowd gathered, so I didn't interrupt, watched and appreciated seeing my worlds collide.

Next to them was someone demonstrating traditional blacksmithing techniques, hammer ringing on anvil. Or urban agriculture projects with vertical gardens and aquaponics systems that could feed a family from a balcony. Handmade clothing and traditional crafts shared space with cutting-edge electronics and experimental art. The juxtaposition of old and new, practical and absurd, serious and playful was constant and delightful.

And then there was the giant cupcake car.

I'm walking between exhibits when it drives past me, an enormous, detailed recreation of a Hostess cupcake, the kind with chocolate cake and black frosting and the white squiggle circles on top. It's big, maybe the size of a go-kart, with a few eye holes for the driver to see out of. I stand there laughing as this perfect cupcake motors past, the driver invisible behind the chocolate frosting facade.

Later I find out the creators rotated drivers, maybe their kids took turns. It doesn't matter who's driving. What matters is that someone looked at the world and thought, "You know what this needs? A drivable cupcake." And then they built it.

At Maker Faire, a giant dessert on wheels is another Saturday.

The lockpicking competition drew me in every year. I'd find myself standing at the edge of the demonstration area, watching the timed competition with fascination. These people were fast, their fingers moving with the kind of muscle memory that comes from thousands of hours of practice. They'd have a lock picked in seconds, sometimes faster than it would take to open it with a key. I'm slow compared to them. I can pick a lock in minutes when I need to, but I don't practice like they do. Watching them reminded me how far dedication can take a skill.

It brought back memories of my high school days when my friends and I would explore the art of getting into places we probably shouldn't have been. There was something deeply satisfying about understanding the mechanics of a lock, feeling the pins set one by one with that subtle click of metal on metal, that moment when everything aligned and the lock gave way. The weight of the picks in your hand. Cold steel with a textured grip. Your breathing slows. Fingers moving with deliberate, fine-motor precision.

The makers running these sessions were generous with their knowledge, patient with beginners, genuinely excited to share what they knew. They'd explain the different types of locks, demonstrate various picking techniques, let people try their hand at practice locks.

The workshops scattered throughout the faire were always packed. I'd direct people toward the soldering station and see parents and kids huddled over circuit boards. The sharp, sweet smell of rosin flux mixing with the acrid, metallic tang of heated solder. The 3D modeling workshop had a constant flow of people watching objects materialize layer by layer. The rhythmic stepper motor music - a series of electronic chirps and whirrs following a predictable pattern. Watching the print head move in a mesmerizing geometric dance, laying down hair-thin lines of molten plastic that harden instantly. You could learn Arduino programming, try your hand at woodworking, understand the basics of welding. The high-pitched whine of power saws. The rhythmic thud-clack of hammers on anvils. Pick up traditional bookbinding skills.

There was a sign for the event I'd been asked to remove, and I needed something sharp to cut through the zip ties or tape. I can't remember which, that I needed a blade and didn't have one.

A police officer was nearby, helping with crowd management as people started to leave. I hesitated. The thought of asking a cop if I could borrow his knife felt terrifying. Would he think I was a threat? Would he say no?

I walked up to him. "Excuse me, could I borrow your pocketknife? I need to remove that sign."

He was chill as hell about it. Didn't even hesitate. Reached into his pocket and handed it over, a cool knife where you pushed a button and the blade flipped open. No questions, no suspicion, one person helping another get a job done.

I used it, finished the cutting, and found him afterwards to return it. He nodded, put it back in his pocket, and we both went about our day. Such a small thing.

The Henry Ford canceled Maker Faire Detroit in 2022, citing sustainability concerns and the significant resources required from staff, volunteers, and partners. The world was different after the pandemic. Priorities had shifted. Resources were stretched thin.

3-10:
The Flow
(2014-2022)

I started improv in 2014. Roller derby had shown me I could be physical. Aerial arts was teaching me I could be strong. Improv was something else entirely.

The first time I got on stage, my hands were shaking. The lights were hot. They created a wall of white that hid the audience. I couldn't see faces. I could hear them.

I had no idea what I was going to say. That was the point.

I went to my first studio and worked through their program. Four intro classes, then Advanced. Scene Work. Long Form. Learning to build something from nothing with another person in real time.

The stage taught me things no class ever had. How to project my voice so it carried past the front row. How to take up space instead of shrinking from it. How to say something and mean it. Twenty years of corporate work had trained me to be measured, careful, quiet. Improv trained me to be loud.

Every show felt like magic. Standing backstage in the wings. People drinking, waiting. Walking out into the lights. Not knowing what would happen next. Trusting my scene partner. Trusting myself. Building something together that had never existed before and would never exist again.

One showcase, we called out to the audience for a famous person suggestion. Someone shouted "Justin Bieber." I had no idea who that was. I committed to whatever I thought it might be. The audience roared. Not because I got it right. Because I fully committed.

I was in Advanced 3 or 4 when it happened.

We'd done a student showcase. Hours had passed. Everyone had gone home. A classmate pulled me aside.

He told me I was holding the troupe back.

I don't remember his exact words. I remember how they landed. Everything I'd been building for two years. Wrong.

I loved these people. I loved being on stage. I loved the flow.

So I left. If I was holding them back, I didn't want to be the reason they couldn't be great.

I cried when I walked away. Absolutely crushed. I'd found something that made me feel alive in ways I'd never felt before. And someone told me I wasn't good enough.

I believed him.

I stopped performing. Weeks went by. The stages I'd been on three nights a week were empty spaces I drove past on the way home.

Then I walked into Pointless.

Pointless was a tiny improv studio started by someone who'd been diagnosed with cancer and decided to build the thing they'd always wanted. Small space. Intimate shows. The kind of place where the back row was ten feet from the stage.

I signed up. Showed up. Got back on stage.

My troupe mates there were wonderful. Different energy than the first studio. Supportive in a way that made the work better, not softer. We built scenes together. Performed together. I found my voice again.

Later, I found out the classmate who'd gutted me had been banned from all the improv studios. Not because of me. Because of a pattern. He'd done this to other people too.

He'd cost me time. Not much else.

My last improv classes were at The Actors Loft. A place in a loft above a car body shop. I took all four of their classes. The Fundamentals of Acting. Character and Scene Study. Improv for Film. Screenwriting the Write Way. Over the years, I did scenes from movies as practice. Crash. Philadelphia. 21 Grams. Traffic. The owner became a friend. I love that place.

We made a movie called "Unicorns Among Us" in the Improv for Film class. Improvised with an outline we all worked on together. Shot in one day. It could all change at any time.

I played Marvin the Marvelous, a very tall character walking on wooden peg stilts through a downtown area. Homemade stilts. Two-by-two wood with bike tires cut up and covering the bottom of the pegs. Excellent traction. Silent steps. I wore long pants that covered the stilts down to the last foot where I'd painted the wood black. Gave me a seven-foot-eleven presence.

I wore a red tailcoat with gold braided epaulets. Ringmaster gear. Heavy fabric that held the sun.

Walking on peg stilts changes everything. You can't stand still. No ankle, those bike tire bottoms. You have to maintain a constant rhythmic stilt-march, a slow pendulous sway. Shifting weight to keep from falling. It made the movement look fluid, like dancing even when standing in place.

Your perspective shifts. Looking over the roofs of cars, across at people sitting in second-story windows. Your balance point moves from your hips to your chest. When you look down, you hinge at the waist. The red tailcoat fans out behind you like wings.

The movie was about a woman who was a unicorn. She cared for the homeless, made construction workers better people. Me, towering and theatrical in my red tails, paired with her at ground level. We healed various characters in the city. All classmates playing different roles. The visual contrast was the point. A physical yes-and.

We filmed on the main street with people walking by. Brick pavers under my stilts. Every recessed grout line, every slightly lifted brick created feedback through the wood into my knees. The click of the rubber peg-tips hitting red brick. Different from concrete. Sharper.

The buildings are two to four stories. At nearly eight feet tall, I was constantly ducking under low-hanging tree branches. Walking at eye-level with people sitting on elevated rooftop patios. The clack of my steps echoed off the glass storefronts. The sound preceded me. People would turn their heads before they saw me.

Since there was no script, everything was reactive. My partner and I had to mind-read each other's movements. If she stopped to heal a space, I circled her like a satellite. If she started a gesture toward someone on the street, I had to yes-and it from seven feet eleven in the air. Maintaining balance while spreading imaginary magic. Flow combining everything from aerial arts and improv.

The guy who told me I wasn't good enough never made a movie.

3-11:
DEER CAMP

(2016-2024)

Nick called me in 2016. "Opening day is November 15th. Rifle season. You'll need a rifle, a deer tag, and hunter safety."

I said yes without thinking about what I was agreeing to.

I had to take hunter safety because I was born after some DNR cutoff date. They held the class at a sporting goods store that specialized in hunting equipment. The instructor was serious about it. Not in a bad way. In a "this will save your life" way.

I don't remember all the laws they taught us. What stuck was the bigger stuff. Safety. Ethics. Responsibility.

You had to demonstrate everything. Proper handling. Safety protocols. All of it. I was nervous as hell during the practical test. But I passed.

When they handed me that Hunter Education Certificate, it felt important. Like I'd earned something. Permission to be in the woods with a weapon. Trust.

That card is still in a drawer somewhere.

Wade showed me to shoot. He'd moved to Michigan from the south. Grew up around guns. He was patient about it. How to hold the rifle. How to breathe. How to squeeze the trigger instead of pulling it. Safety first, always. Muzzle discipline. Finger off the trigger until you're ready.

Nick took me out a few weeks later. He adjusted my stance, watched me breathe through a few rounds. "Wade got you started right," he said. "Now let's tighten up your position." He showed me how his grandfather taught him to distribute his weight, how to make the rifle part of your body instead of something you're holding.

They'd never coordinated. Never compared notes. But somehow Wade's foundation became Nick's starting point, like they'd planned it.

We went to the range to sight in the rifles. Skeet shooting too. Set up like golf but you shot clay discs out of the air with a shotgun. I like to learn about things I don't understand. Learning about firearm types and safety was quite fun.

A family friend sold me a rifle. It became mine. My responsibility.

The property was 300 acres. Nick's family land. Generations of it. We'd take a tractor and 4-wheeler out there to cut trails. Plant crops the animals would eat. Not a food plot to lure them in. A forest where they'd want to be naturally.

I tracked deer through the woods. Read their signs: prints in mud, scat on trails, stripped bark. Moved heel-to-toe to stay quiet. Sat still against trees until the forest forgot I was human.

The first few years, we had 20+ guys spread across multiple cabins. Each cabin would host dinner on rotation. Guys would cook their best meals. Massive stockpot bubbling on a wood-burning stove. Large chunks of turnip, potato, seared meat. Windows fogged over from the heat and steam. I still dream about those steaks. The turkey. The turnip stew. Tacos that were better than they had any right to be.

We'd walk out before sunrise to our tree stands. Metal rungs ice-cold through gloves. Headlamp cutting a small circle of white light through the dark woods. Strap in. Wait until midday. I'd bring a thermos of coffee to stay warm. The cold got into everything. But the coffee helped. The waiting was part of it.

The silence in a tree stand isn't empty. After two hours of sitting motionless, your hearing adjusts. A single leaf falling sounds like a footstep.

CRACK. A sharp, dry snap of a branch from behind my left shoulder. My heart hammers against my ribs. I don't move my head. Just my eyes. Slowly. Grip tightens on the rifle. Safety under my thumb. Waiting for the flash of brown.

A gray squirrel catapults from a low oak limb onto the forest floor. Lands with a heavy thump in the dry leaves. Starts digging furiously.

My heart stays at a gallop for another minute. Eight years, and the squirrels still win the jump-scare every single time.

Come back at lunch. Hang out for a few hours. Watch movies. Head back out for sunset. Return after dark.

It was some of my best memories. A group of guys who often hadn't showered in days. Nothing mattered except showing up. We ate good food. We had good times.

Nick joined the Marines a few years in. After that, the group got smaller. Some years we'd have a dozen guys. Some years, three.

The ritual stayed the same.

I hunted with this group for eight years.

Never saw a deer.

Not one. Eight seasons. Countless hours in tree stands. Coffee going cold. Sunrise after sunrise. The forest moving around me.

Nothing.

I kept going back anyway.

One year, Bob got one.

We field dressed it in the woods. Took the heart back to camp. Held a ceremony. Honored the deer for giving its life. Sliced it thin. Seared it in a cast-iron skillet. Dense, iron-rich. Each of us ate a piece.

It wasn't for show. It was real. An animal died so we could eat. That meant something. Required acknowledgment.

I'd never experienced anything like it. The weight of it. Understanding this wasn't sport. This was sustenance and respect together.

In 2024, I stopped going.

Something set me off one night. I got in my head about it. I left without saying anything.

Walked three miles back to the cabin through a whiteout snowstorm. Wind-driven snow moving horizontally. Filling my tracks within minutes.

They followed my tracks. Three miles through the storm. Back to the cabin.

They had every right to be pissed. I walked into a whiteout alone without telling anyone. They had to follow my tracks to make sure I hadn't died out there.

I haven't been back.

I'm grateful for those eight years.

I never saw a deer.

3-12:
THE CIRCUS OF STRENGTH
(2017-2023)

I saved an email from 2014 for years. It was from an instructor at the aerial studio, responding to my inquiry about an arm-balancing workshop. She was patient and helpful, offering alternatives. Regular classes, privates, times and prices.

I had tried aerial once before, with some friends from roller derby. My body wasn't ready, my brain wasn't ready. It was high up and scary. Everyone was wearing tight clothing. I absolutely hated it. I swore I'd never go back.

That email sat in my inbox for three years. I'd see it every few months while searching for something else. Each time I'd read it again, think about it, and close it. Not yet.

But I kept driving past the studio. That yellow awning on the building. Something about it called to me every time I went through that part of Detroit.

In early 2017, I walked through the door.

You take your shoes off at the door. Black mats cover the floor. Two garage doors that could roll up in summer. An upstairs filled with all kinds of performance equipment we didn't go up there. A colorful bench, a few places to sit when you weren't flying during classes. But you didn't sit to observe. That wasn't what this place was about.

We rotated through instructors. I had two that first day.

I did my research beforehand. Wear tights, cover your armpits. But nothing can truly prepare you for your first real aerial class. I quickly discovered a fundamental problem: I had zero upper body strength. I couldn't even pull myself up onto the trapeze.

The instructor had to give me a boost.

I wasn't surprised. I had to start somewhere.

The fabric. Two long tails hanging from the ceiling. Non-stretch material that felt like high-density bedsheets but with the tensile strength of a tow strap. Professional tissue.

That first night destroyed me. Everything hurt. I could barely move out of bed the next morning.

I remember trying to make eggs. I was eating a lot of eggs because I'd heard the protein was good for recovery. I went to lift my cast iron skillet and physically couldn't do it. My arms wouldn't cooperate.

I gave up and ordered pizza instead. I love pizza. No shame in that.

For the first couple of months, everything hurt. New muscles woke up. Screamed at me.

The standard wrap. First thing you learn with the fabric. You wrap it around your wrist or ankle to create a mechanical advantage. This is where the fabric burn happens. If you slide too fast, the friction creates a stinging heat that can take the top layer of skin right off.

The hip key. The lock that allows you to rest or transition into drops. You use your leg to kick the fabric across your hip bone and roll into it. Creates a secure pivot point. The pressure is immense. Leaves a circus stripe. A deep, horizontal bruise across the hip.

I'd sit in IT meetings with those bruises hidden under my dress pants. The corporate pro on the surface. The aerial athlete underneath.

But the biggest hurdle wasn't physical.

Any time a move required me to fall forward while tied into the fabric, my body remembered the bike accident. It was a flashback. I would freeze, panic. My body would lock up. Primal fear.

The first time it happened, the instructor recognized what was going on. They slowly brought me back into my body. I don't even know how they did it. But they did.

It took weeks before I could do backward drops. My forward drops, I could only do with my eyes closed. And both of them would trigger this nervous laugh that would get more and more intense until the laughter had infected the rest of the room. It was quite fun, .

The first time I did a drop with my eyes closed, I was shocked I did it and lived.

I never got comfortable doing forward drops with my eyes open. Maybe once, a fluke. But mostly, eyes closed was the only way my body would let me do them.

Two months after I started, in March 2017, my aunt died.

Not the heart attack from 2011 that made me leave the law firm. She'd survived that. This time, she didn't.

I was sad. She was full of wisdom and now I had to find it on my own.

I remembered what she'd said after that first heart attack: "Do it now."

What started as one class a week quickly became an obsession. At my height, I was taking eight classes per week. Silks, lyra, straps, hula hoop, aerial pole, even acro yoga where we balanced people on top of people and solved how to make human pyramids. I knew all the instructors, had memorized their teaching styles and favorite warm-ups.

Nobody was there because it was their job. They were there due to their love of the craft. Sage, one of the instructors I worked with one-on-one quite a bit, had done roller derby and various other jobs before aerial. But when she got there, she knew it was her dream.

Aerial was her dream. Nothing will stop her from doing it, absolutely nothing. I haven't met anyone as driven as her. I often think of this when I get stuck in life or feel like it's sludge.

She helped me build my routines. She understood me. She could predict my next move. She knew when something wasn't right, when I wasn't being myself. She would push me harder than anyone else in that studio because she knew I could do it. And she didn't take any of my bullshit.

She would tell me, "You can do anything you put your mind to. Don't forget it."

Many of the instructors also worked as professional performers. They could demo moves all day long and not even break a sweat. It was a level of endurance I didn't know was possible.

Some classes were rough. The conditioning class was like an obstacle course. They'd have five different pieces of equipment up, and they rotated every week. One circuit I remember: pull-ups on the trapeze, climb the straight fabric and touch the top then back down once on each side, flip into a hammock and hold a superman-like pose, push-ups on the floor, then the lyra where you'd flip into an arched position. Lots of squats too. It was great fun.

Then there was contortion class. I would wait until the last minute to go. My body was confused by the splits, couldn't understand what was being asked of it. But we would hold a stretch so long it became story time. We all got to know so much about each other's hilarious moments in their human experience. By the end of class, I felt good. My body felt good.

It was so interesting how each class and instructor had their own style and strengths. So many of them had backstories of trying to be normal. Architects, bankers, all the conventional careers. They were all there by choice.

Some classes you would stay until the very last minute, glowing, not wanting anything to end.

Maybe a month in, I pulled myself onto the trapeze without grunting.

The room erupted. We all clapped and cheered. Often the same people would stay in a series for months at a time, retaking the same class over and over. My class partners and the instructor saw it happen. My own noises of delight made smiles spread through the room.

I was accomplished and excited.

The Russian climb. The most efficient workhorse way to get to the ceiling. You wrap the fabric over the top of one foot and lock it by stepping down with the other. Rhythmic crunch-and-reach motion. Once you master it, you can reach the twenty-five-foot rafters in four or five big strides.

Verbal praise was rare in the studio. A nod from an instructor was a system check: pass. It meant you performed the move correctly. You didn't cheat the physics or rely on sloppy strength.

The studio became my second home. I got stronger.

3-13:
THE PERFORMANCE
(2017-2023)

The showcases started in 2017. Seven total over the next few years.

The first few were in a warehouse event space with concrete floors and industrial lighting. High ceilings, exposed brick walls. Open-plan. You performed just feet away from the front row. You could see the whites of their eyes. You could hear them gasp when you hit the bottom of a drop. There was no backstage. You lived and died in the sight of the audience.

Later, we moved to a real theater with a proper stage. Velvet curtains. Controlled lighting from a technician in a booth. Standing on that stage, the audience is a dark, silent void. The spotlights are so bright they catch the chalk dust floating in the air. You feel isolated, suspended in a column of light, performing for a crowd you can hear but cannot see.

Each time, I'd invite my family. My parents, my aunt, my brother, family friends. They'd show up with smartphones ready, never quite sure what I was going to do but excited to see me try.

The routines got more elaborate each time. I'd work with instructors for months, building sequences that told stories, combining strength moves with dance.

The Russian. Also called a Russian Layback. You wrap the fabric around your waist and one thigh. Then you let go with your hands. Your whole body weight held by the squeeze of the fabric. Twenty feet up. If you don't commit to the lean, you tip. The world goes quiet. The instructors don't cheer. They just watch.

For performances, I wore elaborate costumes that required help to get into. Form-fitting pieces with zippers and fastenings in places I couldn't reach. I remember needing a complete stranger in the bathroom to help me get undressed so I could use the facilities. These weren't simple outfits. They were part of the performance itself.

But the performance that became legendary, the one my family still talks about, was the onesie reveal.

Aerial pole isn't what most people think. It's not club pole dancing. It's legitimate aerial art.

The pole is an 8-foot chrome cylinder rigged to the ceiling. It moves. Swings. Rotates. You need bare skin to stick to it. That's why I shaved my legs. Fabric slides right off chrome. The onesie wouldn't grip.

These events were serious affairs. Families, friends, aerial arts community members filling the seats. Supportive, appreciative atmosphere. Not a place where you'd expect comedy or practical jokes.

My brother had given me this puffy, pink onesie he'd worn to a pajama party. Ridiculous, oversized, the kind of thing I'd wear around the house on cold winter days when maximum coziness was required. Perfect for misdirection.

I was intentionally vague when I invited my family. They knew I was performing, knew I'd been working on something for months. But I didn't provide specifics about the routine or costume.

The setup required one piece of advance work. I'd been asked to film all the routines, which gave me the perfect excuse to position a GoPro to capture audience reaction, not the performance. Nobody thought twice about the camera.

My family arrived, found good seats with a clear view. They weren't making weird faces or looking confused. They knew I was unpredictable. Curious about what I was going to do this time, smartphones ready to document whatever was about to happen.

When it came time for my routine, I made my entrance in that ridiculous pink onesie.

The music started. AronChupa's "Little Swing." Upbeat, playful, perfect.

I reached for the pole and tried to climb it.

In the onesie.

It didn't work. The fabric slid right off the chrome. I looked at it, confused, like I couldn't understand why this wasn't going as planned.

Then the beat dropped.

In one smooth motion, perfectly timed to the music, I stripped off the onesie to reveal my actual performance costume underneath. Silver booty shorts and glittery pasties.

The onesie hit the floor. The crowd erupted. Shouts and howls. My plan was a success.

My mom's brain broke. Her head went crooked. She couldn't process it. Pink pajamas to silver booty shorts to high-strength acrobatics. My aunt reached over and gave her a gentle pat pat.

The routine that followed was one of my best performances. The footage shows it all. Smiles. Everyone laughing, cheering, completely delighted by the whole elaborate setup and the performance that followed.

The shows continued over the next few years. Seven total.

At one of the last shows, I did one of the most difficult routines on the straight fabric. A single piece of fabric hanging from the ceiling, maybe 20 feet up. You climb, wrap yourself in it, drop, spin. If you get tangled wrong or lose your grip, you fall.

At the last practice before the show, I got tied up in the fabric to the point where Sage had to lower me down and untie me. I was stuck.

She told me, "You're going to have to cut this from your routine. Performance etiquette is to do only the things you can do without thinking, things you can do five or six times in a row without breaking a sweat."

On the stage, I was high on the audience's energy. I decided to do my routine as I originally planned. I had one portion that was dangerous. If I got it wrong, I'd be lucky to land in the hospital.

I climbed. Wrapped. Hit every mark. The fabric was tight around my hips and ribs. I could feel the weave pressing into my skin through the costume. The chalk on my hands was drying fast under the lights.

I reached my final position. Twenty feet up. The spotlight was hot on my face. Chalk dust floating in the beam. Below me, the audience was a dark blur of noise.

I had a choice. Drop forward — the move Sage told me to cut. The one I couldn't do five times in practice. The one that got me tangled the day before. Or take the easy exit. Come down the same way I went up. The audience wouldn't know the difference.

I looked down. Two of my instructors were standing in the wings. They knew what I was considering. I could see their faces. They weren't smiling.

The fabric creaked against the rigging point above me. My grip was solid. My wrap was clean. I could do it. I could also miss and fall twenty feet onto a stage.

I took the easy exit. The crowd was ecstatic. They never knew I considered the risk.

I got to the wings. Sage was there. She looked at me with a look that could kill.

I was terrified.

She led me back to the green room where she'd been watching on camera, listening to the crew's radio chatter. She was super upset I took such a risk.

It wasn't anger, at least not at me. She was upset that I did something I shouldn't have done because I couldn't do it in practice. But I did it.

3-14:
THE WALKER
(2018-2020)

The apartment above me had been vacant for a year and a half. Storage for the management company. Then they gutted it. Rebuilt it. Rented it out.

The new tenants left their phone on the hardwood floor.

Every night, footsteps. All hours. The phone would vibrate. They'd walk over to check it. More footsteps. Another buzz. More walking.

I tried writing them a letter. Polite. Reasonable. Explaining the situation.

They didn't speak much English. I never figured out what language they did speak. The letter went nowhere.

That complex had changed. The lady who managed it used to live there. She knew everyone. Asked for our input. Fixed things. Took care of the place.

Then a corporation bought it.

Suddenly we were all just numbers. Service requests went unanswered. The quality of work shifted from "done right" to "good enough for government work."

We watched the building deteriorate around us. Everyone was upset. But nobody seemed able to do anything about it.

I decided I could.

In spring 2018, I moved into a 312 square foot studio downtown.

On moving day, I invited my brother and Cedric, a friend I'd made through the auxiliary who I got dinner with regularly.

I didn't rent a truck. The new place was only half a mile away. How hard could it be?

Cedric didn't even ask. Just took me to U-Haul. They couldn't help us.

We ended up at Home Depot. Got a truck for 90 minutes for $20.

I've never moved so fast in my life.

The new place was five flights up. The first flight was a vertical wall, twice as long as the others because of the high commercial ceilings on the ground floor. The wooden banister was stained dark and worn smooth as glass by a hundred years of hands.

It was hot that day. Really hot.

The four of us hauled everything up those stairs. Boxes, furniture, all of it. By the third flight, my breathing was ragged, echoing off the narrow plaster walls of the stairwell. Sweat made the cardboard boxes feel soft and slick under my fingers. My legs burned. My knees clicked with every step. Racing the 90-minute clock.

By the time we got to my dresser, I looked at it, looked at those stairs, looked at the clock.

"No way in hell."

I started giving things away on the spot. Right there in the alleyway. People walking by got free furniture. The dresser found a new home in about five minutes.

No elevator. Every single day I'd climb those stairs with groceries, laundry, whatever I was carrying.

The studio was tiny. Every inch visible from the center. Kitchen was more of a kitchenette. Bathroom was functional. But it had tall, vertical windows that let in good light and faced the main downtown street where I could watch the world go by. The single-pane glass was thin. During a storm, the glass rattled rhythmically against the wooden tracks. The floor was original hardwood with wide gaps that swallowed dust.

More importantly, it was mine. Quiet. No phones vibrating on hardwood floors above my head. No corporate management that didn't care.

Living in 312 square feet changed how I thought about everything I owned.

The parking garage was blocks away. Four flights of stairs. No elevator.

Every purchase meant carrying it from my car, blocks through downtown, up four flights of stairs, and finding space for it in a studio where space was at a premium.

You stop buying stupid stuff you don't need real quick.

I'd stand in stores holding something, thinking through the whole process. Do I want this enough to carry it? Do I have space for it? What am I getting rid of to make room?

Most of the time, the answer was put it back.

The building had been designed during the Spanish flu days. The heating reflected that era. The radiator hissed and clanked, pushing the room to 90 degrees. The whole system was designed around having your windows open.

Which meant I had my windows open.

Which meant I heard the trains.

Four train crossings in the downtown. Train law required 16 whistle blows total. A loud, mournful sequence that vibrated through the floorboards and into the soles of my feet. All hours of the day and night.

I started setting my schedule by the train whistle. Rarely needed an alarm.

The 11:33 PM train was a low-frequency rumble I felt in my chest. Time for bed. The 6:12 AM whistle was a sharp, high-pitched pierce that cut through the silence of the studio. Time to wake up and get ready for work.

You adapt to whatever environment you're in. Find the rhythm. Make it work.

I started walking.

Not going anywhere specific. Just walking. Every day. Sometimes twice a day. Learning the downtown, the side streets, the shortcuts between buildings.

I'd make my rounds. Coffee shop in the morning. Different route each time. Evening walk after work. The stairs in my building became part of the routine. Four flights up, four flights down. Multiple times a day.

That's when I started noticing the other walkers.

Older guys mostly. Retired. They'd be out exploring the down-town, moving with a slow, rhythmic cadence. They'd stop at specific brick corners to point out the history. Which buildings used to be what. Who owned what business. Where the good deals were.

We'd nod to each other. Eventually we'd stop and talk. Eyes scanning the architecture rather than the sidewalk.

I became one of them. The walkers. The guys who knew the downtown because we walked it every day.

That's also when I found the $5 burger night.

This was back when $5 burger nights were still a thing. You had to buy a drink. That was the deal. But burgers were good and the place had a vibe. The air was heavy with the scent of seared beef and cold beer. A low, steady hum of voices.

I started going regularly.

The bartender was Emily. She had this gift. She'd look around the bar, see who was there, and somehow know exactly who should meet who. She'd introduce people, moving with a social rhythm, bridging the gaps between strangers. She'd suggest they sit together. Mix people up to maximize fun.

Before I knew it, she'd assembled a crew.

There was the retired philosopher. Decades of teaching, still loved talking ideas, still curious about everything.

The graphic designer who'd been doing it for over 40 years. He'd seen the entire evolution of the industry. From paste-up boards to digital. Still loved the work.

The cybersecurity business owner. Smart as hell. We'd compare notes on tech stuff, trade stories about the industry.

The movie buff. That guy had seen everything. Could quote anything. Had opinions on directors I'd never even heard of.

And me.

We'd show up on burger night. Emily would have our drinks ready. We'd talk about everything. Work, life, movies, philosophy, technology, whatever came up.

Sometimes Emily would join us on her nights off. We'd hit estate sales together. I'd been going to estate sales for years. Hundreds of them. It's a fun pastime for me. Seeing how people lived. What they kept. What they valued.

She had the same curiosity.

We'd wander through strangers' houses, looking at their stuff, imagining their stories. Sometimes we'd buy things. Sometimes we'd just look.

I remember one conversation at the bar, right before lockdown. We were talking about masks.

Not medical masks. Fashion masks. How they could become a statement. A status symbol. Like designer sunglasses or watches.

None of us wore masks yet. They were still just a concept. Something we were watching happen in other countries. Something we thought might come here but weren't sure.

We had no idea.

Just before lockdown, I put on my stilts and grabbed a bundle of sage. Walked the downtown like that. Tall. Smoking sage. Just to see what would happen.

People loved it. Stopped to talk. Asked questions. Took photos.

Little did I know this was going to turn into weekly costumes.

When pandemic hit, the entire downtown went silent.

I'd stand at my window and look out over the street. Empty. Completely empty. As far as I could see, no one.

The restaurants closed. The coffee shops closed. The bars closed. Everything closed.

The animals came back.

Birds everywhere. So many birds. They'd taken over the downtown again. Landing on empty tables outside restaurants. Perching on street signs. Walking down the middle of the street like they owned the place.

Which they did. For a while.

I stopped going outside as much. What was the point? Everything was closed. Everyone was inside.

Days blurred together. I'd work from home. Stare at screens. Walk to the window. Stare at empty streets. Walk back to screens.

One evening, Dawn called.

We'd met at aerial pole class before lockdown. She was the person us newbies would go to when we needed someone to show us a move. Skill and patience. Natural teacher.

We'd gotten coffee once. Talked until her parking meter ran out. Then lockdown happened and we'd been checking in over the phone.

"How are you doing?" she asked.

"Fine," I said.

There was a pause. "You sound like you're being tortured."

I laughed. Sort of. "No, I'm fine."

"Go outside," she said. "Touch grass. Actually touch it. You need to go outside."

I looked at my window. The empty street. The birds.

"Yeah," I said. "Yeah, this is better."

I walked down to a nearby park. Found green grass. Actually touched it.

Dawn called one evening.

During the pandemic, I moved from the studio to a loft.

Three door walls. Tons of airflow. A pool for the ten units. Still walking distance of the downtown but far enough away that I no longer heard the drunks walking by at 2 AM.

It was a great deal. Heat included. AC unit in the wall. The washer and dryer were shared. One set for ten units. A bit strange but we all communicated, coordinated, made it work.

I kept walking. Even when the downtown was empty. Even when there was nowhere to go.

The walkers found each other again eventually. Different spots. Outdoor spaces. Parks. We'd see each other from a distance, wave, keep moving.

But I kept walking.

3-15:
THE GREAT AMERICAN ROAD TRIP
(2020)

The 312-square-foot studio apartment had seemed perfectly reasonable when I'd signed the lease in February 2020. "I'll only be here to sleep," I'd told the property manager, excited about being downtown. Six weeks later, it became my entire world.

Three laptops balanced on a kitchen table meant for two people. Two monitors for the utility company job, one personal laptop for sanity. I'd bounce between all three all day long, the blue light burning into my retinas, my world shrinking to the size of multiple screens. My job was to watch everything, prevent problems before they became disasters, stay invisible while keeping systems running for thousands of people who'd never know I existed.

The first five days of lockdown, I didn't go outside once. Not even to check the mail. I worked, slept, worked, made food, worked. The cycle was hypnotic in its simplicity. Safe in its predictability. Soul-crushing in its sameness.

By day five, I was getting cabin fever and wanted to go outside. When I looked out my window, there wasn't a person as far as I could see. My body had started to mold into the shape of my office chair: shoulders rounded, neck craned forward, lower back screaming.

Dawn called me in the evening of day five. "How are you doing?" she asked.

"Fine," I croaked. "Working."

There was a long pause. Then: "Tom, you sound like a prisoner on death row. When's the last time you went outside?"

I had to think about it. The fact that I had to think about it was the answer.

"Go outside," she commanded. "Right now. While I'm on the phone. I need to hear you breathing real air."

I laughed, it came out as more of a cough, but I did it. Walked down the five flights of stairs, pushed open the door to the sidewalk, and stood there blinking in the afternoon sun like some kind of cave creature. The air smelled different. Alive. I'd forgotten the air could smell alive.

"Better?" she asked.

"Yeah," I said, and my voice already sounded more human. "Yeah, this is better." I walked down the street to a nearby park to touch the green grass.

That phone call saved me from completely disappearing into the digital world. But even with daily walks added to my routine, the apartment felt smaller every day. I'd pace the five steps from kitchen to bedroom area, turn around, pace back. Five steps. Turn. Five steps. Turn. Like a tiger in a too-small zoo enclosure.

The walls started feeling like they were breathing, expanding and contracting with my own breath. I'd catch myself having full conversations with my laptops, thanking them for working, apologizing when I had to restart them. The isolation was doing something to my brain.

My supervisor noticed before I did. He's a good man, the kind who pays attention to his people. One day in July, he messaged me: "Your vacation bank is high. You need to take some time."

It wasn't a suggestion. It was a concern dressed as management speak.

I left Michigan in July of 2020, setting out for a new adventure, ready to find beauty along the way. I could work from anywhere. I had to prove it to myself.

I loaded my silver sedan, six-speed manual transmission, with a cooler full of food, my three laptops and mobile hotspot, and the tiny tent my brother had nicknamed "the coffin tent." The stick shift required a constant, four-limb conversation with the machine. I felt the mechanical thrum of the engine through the gear knob in my palm. The delicate teeter-totter dance between my left foot releasing the clutch and my right foot pressing the gas. When I hit the friction point, the car shuddered slightly - a physical signal that the engine was biting. The smooth, gliding snick of a perfect upshift on an open road.

My car had WiFi built in. I had a MiFi device. At campgrounds, I'd combine my hotspot with their WiFi to ensure I had a reliable connection. During meetings, I'd layer all three connections together. Some days I'd run my car the entire day to keep the connection alive while camping. I had to be ready at a moment's notice. Nobody could know I was traveling.

The SS Badger ferry took me across Lake Michigan, a four-hour crossing from Ludington, Michigan, to Manitowoc, Wisconsin, covering 62 miles. The last coal-fired passenger vessel operating on the Great Lakes, designated a National Historic Landmark, it was running on a seasonal basis with all its games and amenities closed for the pandemic.

A massive steel platform vibrating with the deep, rhythmic chug of marine diesel engines. The deck plates hummed under my boots. The railing was cold, slick with salt spray, vibrating with enough intensity to make my forearms tingle when I leaned on it.

It was empty. Maybe thirty to forty vehicles followed by a few semi-trucks. Lots of bikers, but we were all spaced apart, masks required indoors. We left the dock and after a half hour we lost all phone service crossing the lake. I would have to check when I got to the other side if anyone had called.

The steamship was like going back in time. Everything about it felt vintage, from the wood paneling to the massive engines you could watch working below deck. In the middle of the lake, there was no phone service, no nothing. The air was a sharp, bracing cold that tasted of salt and wet iron. The water was a dark, churning slate gray, capped with white foam that hissed as the hull cut through it. The smell was a heavy mix of fish, diesel exhaust, and open-ocean vastness. It was us and water as far as one could see, bright sunlight reflecting off the waves. I spent most of my time walking the deck and lying on it, soaking in the beautiful sunny day, social distancing from the handful of other passengers who'd decided crossing a Great Lake was worth the risk.

It was the first time I'd been unreachable in months. Four hours of no connection. The perfect bridge from my old life into travel mode. I hadn't realized how much I needed that, the physical act of crossing water, of putting distance between me and everything I'd been, of being completely unavailable even if someone needed me. The world kept turning without me for four hours, and nothing broke.

Wisconsin unfolded into a landscape I didn't know existed, a place where southwestern Wisconsin meets southeastern Minnesota, northeastern Iowa, and the northwestern corner of Illinois, a region the locals called the Driftless Area or Bluff Country. Rolling hills carved by hands instead of glaciers, valleys that shouldn't exist in the Midwest.

A farm-to-table campground became my home base for the first few days. An organic farm during the week, it had campsites scattered by the garden. A few farm dogs appointed themselves my guides, following me around as I explored. The kindness of everyone there set the tone for the entire trip.

Steven, a guy who lived behind the farm in concrete domes he'd built himself, found me and talked to me. The farm-to-table campground people had told him about my story starting, about me working remotely and traveling during the pandemic. He invited me over to see what he'd created. I got to experience it firsthand: the meditation room that made you want to meditate, the kitchen that made you chatty, the bathroom that relaxed your entire body. Each room held its own energy, distinct and intentional.

He told me about tracking down an energy shift in the area, how it led him to Kinstone. He drew me a map on a napkin, his directions careful and specific.

After Steven gave me those handwritten directions, I drove to Kinstone. I have it on video. I'm yelling "oh my god" over and over because every direction in that area is a level of beauty I never knew existed on earth. Kinstone sat on thirty acres in Fountain City, a modern megalithic garden with standing stones arranged in circles, a labyrinth, and a cordwood chapel with liquor bottles pressed into the walls to let sunlight through in colored fragments. Amy, the woman who'd created it, met me as I arrived, welcoming me like she'd been expecting me. She'd retired from making power meters, the exact same meters my company used, and left that life behind completely.

"I don't even remember that life anymore," she said. "Once I opened this space, everything else faded."

I walked the grounds for hours. The stone circles. The labyrinth. The chapel.

I drove east from Wisconsin, watching the landscape transform. I was starting to notice the pattern. Every state I crossed, someone would warn me about the next one. "Watch out when you get to Idaho, those people are shady." Then in Idaho: "Montana's where you gotta be careful."

I met nothing but kindness. When I pulled over too long in the backcountry with no GPS, no phone, no AM or FM radio, a paper map, it wouldn't take more than ten minutes for a pickup truck to appear. "You okay? Need directions? Engine trouble?" People checking, offering, helping. On a number of occasions, Native Americans invited me to camp on their land, fed me, and treated me like I was expected.

Everyone has a story. You have to ask questions.

Sometimes you don't even have to ask questions; the story finds you. I was in a laundromat in some small town, passing the time on a hot day while my clothes tumbled dry. The air was thick with the smell of detergent and dryer sheets, and the front door was propped open for airflow. A woman came in like a storm, yelling at everyone. She was being super rude, moving through the space and finding something to insult each patron about. She was clearly looking for a fight. I watched from my chair, pretending to be absorbed in my book.

She went outside, lit a cigarette, and started ranting on the phone to her son about how everyone inside was horrible. We could hear every word. When she finished, she opened the door to come back in, and everyone in the room braced for things to escalate. But they didn't. Instead, she went to each person she had insulted and apologized directly. She told us her daughter was in the hospital, and that she was at her wit's end. The entire energy of the room shifted in an instant. It ended with strangers hugging strangers, everyone there listening to her, all of us doing our best to support someone during a very difficult time.

In Denver, I stopped to visit Chloe, a friend who'd moved from Detroit a year or two prior. We hit estate sales together and she told me she was looking at apartments, so I went with her. It fascinated me how different yet the same they were in Denver as they were in Detroit.

Montana opened up into the endless sky. At a ranch spanning twenty square miles, I met a cattle farmer who used to be a vegetarian. It was pandemic time, and people were extra chatty after being isolated. She'd changed her entire life, gave up vegetarianism, because she needed to know her cattle were taken care of properly, that they had a name instead of a number and a good life before the end.

In Idaho, in the Hoodoo Mountains, I found treehouses. The owner was a huge inspiration. On a business trip, she sat next to an exhausted businessman who told her, "Whatever you do, don't live a life like me." She quit her corporate job, bought land, and built a magical space. One of her last texts to me, before she passed away a couple of years ago, is a message I carry with me always. She told me to trust the sweat lodge, to trust the people around me, and to trust that I was able to be aware of more than I could ever imagine, if I stopped pretending I couldn't see it.

That night, I set up my coffin tent in the designated camping area. Low-profile, one-person shelter. The fabric was thin, crinkly nylon that magnified every sound. Heavy footsteps and breathing circled my tent. Mama moose and her baby. I slid into the tent like a drawer, lying perfectly flat, shoulders pinned by the narrow walls. The ceiling was only inches from my face. I lay perfectly still in the darkness, terrified. The tent windows opened from the outside, so I couldn't see what was happening. Every rustle of the nylon sounded massive. I put on my headphones and played an episode of Rick and Morty, something familiar to keep my brain from panicking. In the morning, they were gone. A woman camping nearby showed me a picture she'd taken. The moose was the size of a small truck. They'd been close enough to have stepped on my tent if they'd wanted to.

The days blurred together. I'd been driving for sixteen hours one night when a friend back home, who could see my location, called me on the phone and used her mom's voice: "There's a town coming up. I found you a hotel. It's time for you to rest." The town had a rodeo going on. I got one of the last rooms. I explored the town, where boots with spurs were a common sight. I got dinner, then walked back to my hotel, grateful to be horizontal in a safe place.

Day nineteen or twenty, I'd lost track, I pulled over at a viewpoint on the Continental Divide. The sky was a deep, bruised indigo. The clouds seemed low enough to touch. The air was thin - every breath felt like it was missing something, forcing me to take deeper, more conscious inhales. My skin felt tight and dry from the high-altitude wind. An absolute, ringing silence broken only by the snap of my jacket fabric in the wind and the crunch of gravel under my boots. The beauty stretched out in every direction, massive and indifferent and exactly what I needed to see. The landscape felt stretched - vast, jagged peaks that made my sedan feel like a small, insignificant speck of dust on a massive rock.

I stood there for a long time.

I can handle this, I thought. I can go anywhere and be safe and happy.

Twenty-two days. Eighty-five hundred miles. Fifteen states. Stars I didn't know existed.

When I got back to Michigan, Dawn and I met up to swap stories. Her hands were calloused from farmwork. Mine were tight from gripping a steering wheel for three weeks. We both looked different, tanned, tired, alive in a way we hadn't been before leaving.

3-16:
THE LAND OF ENCHANTMENT
(2020)

I was in New Mexico, and I knew I was in for a cold night. The air was thin and electric, carrying the scent of parched earth and the medicinal, peppery smell of crushed sagebrush. The wind was a dry, constant pressure that pulled moisture from my lips and eyes. The silence wasn't empty - it was a heavy, ancient presence that rang in my ears.

I'd reserved a spot at a campground with a power plug so I wouldn't freeze while I slept. When I arrived at the gated entrance, a tiny city in the middle of the desert next to the Rio Grande, there was a whiteboard: "Call this number and ask for Jim."

I dialed the Pennsylvania number. Jim answered and told me to meet him at the local bar. "I'm from the north," he said. "You'll be able to find me."

I walked down the street and into the first bar I saw. The building was pure New Mexico: vibrant colors, local art on the walls, a mix of travelers and locals creating that easy energy you only find in places where people come to escape or discover something. Everyone except one guy wearing a sports jersey. I zeroed in on him like I was on a spy mission. "You must be Jim."

We had a beer. He told me about retiring and working campgrounds for months at a time, learning to fit into different parts of the country. "You're going to like this one," he said. "There are rooms with tubs. Two taps: one is hot spring water, one is city water. You mix them to get the temperature right. An hour in there, nothing in your body will hurt anymore. Close as you'll get to a fountain of youth."

We laughed, finished our drinks, and he got me checked in and hooked up to power. He was right about the cold. Temperature was already dropping from the 80s into what would be a freezing night in the 30s.

I explored the campground and found the tubs. Private rooms for one or two people, and a large public tub that could hold half a dozen. In the public tub, two women and a kid were talking to another man. I watched the way they moved the water with their hands, the way the man seemed to be unwinding from something heavy.

A friend had told me before I left: "In the next town, you're going to meet two women travelers that have a bit of magic to them."

I knew immediately. These were them.

I put my swimsuit on and joined them. We connected instantly. Over the next three days, our group kept expanding:

people from Michigan, Tennessee, Florida, Colorado, Germany, Pennsylvania, New Mexico. All ages, all walks of life, all drawn to the same temporary community.

That first night, I walked the campground inviting people to a fire. Why not host one? The youngest person who came was fifteen with her mom. The oldest was a seventy-five-year-old woman who'd sold everything she owned to find herself. The stories ranged from a grandmother asking how to be respectful of her transgender grandchild, to a van-lifer whose dad had dangerously rewired her van. A few of us who knew wiring offered to take a look the next day.

For three days, we hung out nonstop. Jim even gave me a bottle of limoncello to share. It was a magical little community forged in hot spring water and campfire stories.

Eventually, everyone split up, back to their own realities or onwards to their next adventure. I had an Airbnb waiting for me, so remote in the mountains that the host had warned me ahead of time: "Top off your fuel and bring food. The nearest store is 72 miles away. The nearest neighbor is 6 miles away."

I got there, unloaded essentials from the van into the cabin, and went to move the van to a better spot. The horizon stretched so far it felt like I could see the curvature of the earth. The sky was a blue so deep it was almost purple, meeting the jagged, flat-topped mesas that looked like purple shadows in the distance. Stepping out of the van, I felt the immediate zap of static electricity. The pressure in my ears shifted. My lungs worked harder, the air feeling crisp and empty of humidity. The ping-ping-ping of Waldo's cooling engine was the only sound in a landscape that seemed to swallow noise.

It got stuck. Completely stuck. I texted the host on the impossibly slow satellite Wi-Fi. They could be there to pull me out in three days.

"Awesome," I replied. "I'm not going anywhere. I've got enough supplies."

This was when I truly disconnected. They don't call New Mexico "The Land of Enchantment" for no reason. Every night, the stars were unbelievable. An overwhelming, three-dimensional dome. Without the city lights of Michigan, the stars weren't just points of light - they were thick, textured clouds of silver. The cold at night was a physical weight. A dry cold that settled into my marrow. The darkness beyond the cabin fence was filled with noises: coyotes, maybe other things I couldn't identify. If I howled at the stars, I'd get responses from multiple directions.

Something felt like it was pulling me off into the woods at night, but I refused out of fear. Not yet.

On the second to last morning my phone buzzed: 'Call this number.'

It was a manager from an old job. I hiked to the only spot with cell service, a bench on the side of a cliff. I made the call.

Mike had died. Days before my trip. "Ecto-1," as we called him in roller derby. We'd worked together before he joined derby because of me. He saw what it was doing for me and wanted in. He was one of those people who could light up a room by walking in. At work, he handled incidents, gathering teams, coordinating resolution of issues, always making the chaos feel manageable. I'd seen him a year ago at his 41st birthday party.

The shock hit first, then the sadness. Then something else, a complicated grief layered with old wounds.

I'd been removed from the derby Facebook groups when my membership lapsed. It was abrupt, and I couldn't see the posts they were making about Mike. But a friend told me they were remembering how they'd loved Ecto.

And now he was gone, and I couldn't even be part of the community mourning for him.

I sat on that cliff bench for a long time after the call ended. The view stretched for miles: desert, mountains, sky. I let a few people know, then made my way back to the cabin.

That night, I knew my answer to the woods had changed. Life is short. Too short. Mike was forty-one.

No matter what was out there, I was going on that hike.

I made food, read, worked the fire in the wood stove. The click-click-whoosh of the propane stove ignition. The flame was a transparent, flickering blue that struggled slightly in the thin air. The sudden bloom of heat against my face - a sharp contrast to the biting chill of the desert morning. Once night fell, I geared up and went.

The night was different, silent in a way that felt intentional. I walked carefully, using my flashlight to find the cairns marking the trail. Small piles of stones to make sure I didn't walk off the cliff.

When I reached the bench, a coyote was sitting there. sitting. Watching my flashlight.

I froze.

Coyotes are pack animals. They don't sit alone like this. It made no sense.

We stared at each other. What felt like hours was probably only a few minutes. I wish I could say I'd taken drugs or had been drinking, because what happened next is hard to explain without sounding like I've lost my mind.

But I was completely sober. And something was happening.

Something shifted in me. Not words, deeper than that. A knowing. I'd been carrying this idea that to be strong, I had to fit a certain mold. But the Native men of this land, long hair, bright colors on their tribal outfits and clothing, deeply connected to nature, they didn't fit any mold. They were sensitive and strong. Different and powerful.

I didn't have to look like them to share that spirit. I didn't have to be anything other than what I was.

The coyote bowed its head to me.

Without thinking, I bowed back. Pure instinct. I wasn't deciding anything. I was an observer in my own body, responding to something I didn't fully understand.

Then the silence shattered. Howling erupted from all around me. The pack was looking for their missing member, and I was standing in the middle of it.

Time to run.

I took off through the woods, adrenaline spiking, surrounded by the sounds of the pack communicating in the darkness. I remembered the Native American man I'd met at a gas station a few days earlier. He'd welcomed me to the area, we'd chatted briefly, and then he'd said something strange: "I know you're going to be okay." I'd dismissed it as friendly conversation.

Now it felt like a prophecy.

I fell, scrambled back up, used my flashlight to find the cairns. The nature that had been silent was now intensely alive.

For a city guy like me, it was overwhelming. Every sound felt like it was right behind me.

I saw the cabin's fence and ran harder, jumping over it and slamming the door behind me. I sat on the floor by the wood stove, breathing hard. The smell of pine burning in the stove started to calm me down.

Then I looked at myself. I had cactus needles stuck all over my body, right through my clothes.

A few days earlier, the camp host at the hot springs had gotten poked by a thorn. He'd shown me how to remove it: "Push inwards, then pull out." He'd demonstrated, getting a little blood. "I don't know why I showed you that."

Now I knew why.

I grabbed a bowl and started pulling thorns out, one by one. They didn't bleed much.

After I'd removed them all, I loaded up the stove, showered, and made tea. But I didn't eat right away. I sat by the window, listening to the howls of the pack. It sounded like they were doing roll call, finding each other, confirming everyone was accounted for. They'd found their missing member.

I sat there warming up.

When we finally met in Vegas, Dawn and Jade both flew out. The chemistry between me and Dawn was different. Stronger. We were a thousand miles from home.

3-17:
THE COFFEE SHOP
(2020)

I met Dawn in an aerial pole class a couple years into doing aerial.

She was the person us newbies would go to when we needed someone to show us a move. We'd skip the instructor and go straight to Dawn. She had that rare combination of skill and patience that made her a natural teacher. She'd demonstrate the move slowly, break it down into parts, wait while you figured it out.

One day I went to grab my stuff from the cubby by the door. My water bottle. My shoes. The usual end of class routine.

To my own shock, I announced to the room, "Does anyone want to grab a coffee?"

The words came out before I'd thought about them. Louder than I'd meant. Everyone in the changing area heard.

Dawn said yes.

The coffee shop was in my town. Walking distance from my apartment. I parked at home and walked up the street, checking my phone to see how far out she was. By the time Dawn arrived, I was already inside scoping out seats.

The place was clean and modern. One side had tables where people sat laughing and talking. Another line of booth tables where people worked on laptops. Sofas over there. More sofas on the other side with more tables.

We found a booth by the fireplace. The fire wasn't on yet. Too early in the season. But the spot felt private. Protected.

We didn't get coffee. Tea maybe. Macarons. Those little circle things that are really tasty and fall apart if you look at them wrong. I can never remember how to say it right.

I don't remember what we talked about at first. Life probably. The usual surface stuff you cover when you're getting to know someone. Where you're from. What you do for work. The safe topics.

Then it went deeper.

The world as each of us saw it. What we believed. What scared us. What didn't.

She was different.

Nothing I said scared her. I could talk about life and she was interested to learn more. She'd ask questions that made me think. Questions I hadn't asked myself. She didn't try to fix anything or offer advice. She listened. Really listened. The kind of listening where you know someone is actually hearing you, not waiting for their turn to talk.

Then she started talking about her life.

Former model. Someone that's done things. Someone that's been published on a book cover. She had stories about photoshoots and travel and a whole world I knew nothing about. So cool. So different from anyone I'd been spending time with.

We showed each other pictures of costumes we both had. Different outfits we'd collected over the years. She had way more than I did. All kinds of pieces. Vintage finds. Things she'd made herself. Her eyes lit up talking about them.

The conversation flowed. No awkward pauses. No struggling to find things to say.

Before we knew it, her phone dinged.

Parking meter. Time was up.

"I should go," she said.

But neither of us moved right away. We kept talking. Standing now. Jackets on but not leaving. That thing where you know you need to go but you're not quite ready for the conversation to end.

I walked with her to her car. It was on my way home to my apartment. We kept talking the whole way. Finally said goodbye. Went our separate ways.

I walked the rest of the way home thinking about how different that had been from most coffee meetings. How easy it felt.

GRiZMAS came up a few weeks later. Roller disco prom disco edition. Special event at the rink.

I wore a neon orange suit. The one that makes people's eyes hurt if they look at it too long.

Dawn wore a neon dress. Equally bright. Equally impossible to ignore.

A couple of her friends came with her. All of us in various levels of costume and holiday cheer.

The rink was packed. More people than I'd ever seen there. The music was loud. Holiday songs remixed with electronic beats. The strobe lights made everything feel like a music video.

We were the most outrageous people there. Glowing neon in a sea of regular clothes. There's a video on Facebook somewhere. We're in it for maybe a second of screen time. But you can definitely spot us.

Here's the thing though.

When we were on the rink going in circles, we'd lose each other constantly. The crowd was that thick. That chaotic. People cutting across. Couples holding hands and taking up space. Everyone moving at different speeds.

I'd be skating along and suddenly Dawn would be gone. I'd have to slow down. Speed up. Scan the crowd. Finally spot that neon dress three people ahead or five people behind. Work my way over to her.

She'd be doing the same thing. Looking for neon orange in the chaos.

We'd find each other. Laugh. Skate together for a few minutes. Then lose each other again.

The two brightest people in the building, constantly losing each other in the crowd.

At some point after that, Dawn told me she'd been teaching herself to skate at home.

"I marked circles on my floor," she said. "Watched YouTube videos. Practiced the moves."

She'd done it all on her hardwood floor in her condo. Tape marking out the paths. Hours of practice while watching tutorials. Teaching herself the techniques.

She's a gardener. Needs to keep her body healthy to do her work. "I should probably get proper safety gear," she said.

"I know a good shop if you've got an afternoon," I said. "I'll take you."

We went to a skate shop downriver the next week. Part anime shop, part skate shop. Posters of characters I didn't recognize covering one wall. Skates and pads and wheels covering the other. Run by a couple of skaters from the local derby team.

Dawn walked in with purpose. She'd done her research. Knew what she was looking for.

She's smart. She figures things out. I hung back because this was her thing, but also because Dawn doesn't need someone hovering. She's got it.

Dawn found some knee pads and elbow pads on the mid-level shelf. Checked the price tags. Did the math in her head. Nodded to herself.

The clerk watched this. Walked over.

"No no no," the clerk said. Not mean. Matter of fact. "You don't want those."

She pointed down. Lower shelf. Different brand.

"Look a little bit lower."

Dawn picked up the ones the clerk was pointing at. Heavier. Better construction. Only a couple dollars more.

"Those ones are like falling on a kitten," the clerk said. Her face completely serious. "Very soft."

Derby humor. Dark jokes delivered deadpan. The kind of thing that sounds insane to outsiders but makes perfect sense if you know.

Dawn laughed. Bought the better pads.

We went to the roller rink the following week.

The wooden floor had been there since I was a kid. Same boards. Same scuff marks from decades of wheels. The place felt like a time capsule. Some of the strobe lights were original equipment. The kind they don't make anymore. That specific quality of light that takes you right back to elementary school field trips.

We laced up our skates at the benches. Dawn was faster at it now. She'd been practicing that too apparently.

The smell hit when we rolled onto the floor. Pizza. Birthday party somewhere in the building. That combination of grease and cheese and cardboard that means kids are having the best day of their lives.

Dawn was good. Really good for someone who'd taught herself at home with YouTube videos and tape on the floor. She had her balance. Her posture. The basic mechanics were solid.

I'd invited my derby friend to come skate with us. She hadn't skated in a while and it would be good to have her around. When she showed up, we moved to the practice area to work on the important stuff.

The most critical thing in derby is learning to fall if anything feels wrong or off. You don't doubt it. You go to a knee to prevent injury. Derby trains you to go to your knee as a fail-safe. Sometimes trying to save yourself after going too far into a move could risk injury. Better to take the knee.

We armed Dawn with her super thick knee pads and started drilling.

"Left knee," I called out.

Dawn dropped. Got back up.

"Right knee."

Down. Up.

"Left. Right. Left. Right."

Over and over. Getting up in between each time. Making her body download the muscle memory. In real derby practice you'd hear the whistle. One blow meant take a knee no matter what you were doing. Two blows meant switch knees. We didn't use a whistle at a public rink, but the drill was the same.

Repetitions. That's what it takes. You can't learn it quickly. The body needs to practice it until it becomes automatic. Until you don't think about it anymore.

Then we moved on to crossovers.

We were in the corner where the practice section meets the huge rink. Like getting on the expressway, except every lane is the fast lane. We'd been playing in the practice area, going back and forth, but Dawn needed more space to really open up full throttle.

The main rink was packed. Skaters everywhere. But then the birthday party called all the kids in for cake, and suddenly we had a bit more space to ourselves.

"Okay," I said. *"Crossovers. You're going to cross your right foot over your left to gain speed through the turn."*

I demonstrated. My derby friend demonstrated. Both of us showing the motion.

Dawn looked like a baby deer. That thing where you don't know how your legs work, but on wheels instead of ice. That's all of us when we're getting started. A rite of passage.

"Bend your knees," my friend said.

Dawn bent them. A little.

"More," I said.

She bent them more. Still not enough. But that's how it goes. The first few rounds you think you're bending them but you really aren't. Just a tiny bit. You can always go more bent.

Dawn tried the crossover.

Her legs got tangled. Weight distribution all wrong. She caught herself before falling.

"Again," my friend said. "Lower."

Second try. Better. Noticeably better. She was actually getting low now. The crossover was smoother but still hesitant. Still thinking too much about the mechanics.

"One more time," I said. "Don't think. Just do it."

Third try.

She got it.

The weight transfer clicked. The motion flowed. Her body understood what her brain had been trying to tell it. She came out of the corner with speed, actually accelerating through the turn instead of fighting it.

I started laughing. I couldn't help it.

Three tries. Three tries and she'd improved as much as I did in three weeks.

"What?" Dawn asked, skating back over.

"Nothing," I said, still laughing. "You're just ridiculously determined."

That's Dawn though. That determination. That creativity where nothing stops her. She sees something, decides she's going to learn it, and then she does.

My derby friend nodded. "Great progress," she said.

Derby people have seen everything. But even she was impressed.

We worked on stops next. T-stops where you drag one foot perpendicular behind you. Plow stops where you push your feet out and use the inside edges to slow down. Each one requiring different muscle memory, different balance points. More repetitions. More corrections. More of Dawn's body learning what to do without her having to think about it.

We kept skating after she was gone. The pizza smell faded as the birthday party cleared out. The kids thinned. The rink got quieter. Just the music and the sound of wheels on wood and the occasional laugh from other skaters.

We went ice skating at some point too.

It felt unfamiliar to be on ice outdoors with the holiday lights above us. We were the only people on the rink. Late. Had the place to ourselves. The blades instead of wheels changed everything about balance and movement. Different physics entirely. Not dangerous. Strange. Beautiful though, skating under those lights with nobody else around.

She lived near my work, so it was easy to stop over on the way home. I started doing that maybe once a week. We'd get dinner somewhere. Talk about life. Watch a movie. Just hang out. No agenda. Just spending time together because it was easy and fun.

That's when things started getting unusual at work.

Lots of suits around the facility I was in. More than usual. Lots of officials. Walking around. Having meetings behind closed doors. People looking serious.

We knew something was up.

I was telling Dawn about it. How strange things felt. How the energy had shifted.

My work activated their pandemic protocol. This was the start of 2020's global pandemic. They asked for volunteers for the bunker list. I figured I didn't have any kids or anybody to take care of, so why not. I didn't know exactly what that meant. It had changed a lot over time. But it meant I might be losing my freedom for a while in order to protect infrastructure digitally. Plan for the worst.

I called Dawn as soon as I could. "Go grocery shopping. I can't tell you any more. But get everything you need for at least two weeks."

She didn't ask questions. She listened. Trusted me.

We both went to the stores. Stocked up. Got ahead of the rush that would come a few days later when everyone else figured it out.

Then we locked down.

Separate homes. Separate lives. Watching the world shut down from different windows.

Her world was plants. Everywhere. All kinds and sizes. Succulents on the windowsill. Hanging plants from the ceiling. A huge ALOE. A Fern. So many others I had no clue what they were.

She had the upper floor of her building. Warm and cozy. A ton of natural light coming in from a window that overlooked a courtyard. The light changed throughout the day, moving across her hardwood floor, catching the leaves of all those plants.

It smelled like incense. Always. That sweet smoke smell that sticks to fabric and makes a space feel like it belongs to someone specific.

Sounds were quiet inside. But during pandemic, the nearby gym started doing outdoor classes. You'd hear their workout clock start at random times. Beep beep beep. Then counting down. Then silence again. This weird punctuation to the still-ness of her condo.

A purple freezer with two giant googly eyes on the door. Actual googly eyes. The kind you glue onto craft projects. They moved when you opened the door. Made you smile every single time.

She had a hydroponic system where she grew kale. The kale just kept growing over and over again, repopulating itself. I was fascinated by this. She had a compost system too. All her food scraps went into it. She really thinks about this stuff. That's the reason I have reusable grocery bags and a little holster ready to go now.

Mid century modern furniture she'd found at estate sales and thrift stores over the years. Each piece with a story. Hardwood floor with skate circles marked out in blue painter's tape. A pole for aerial practice bolted into a ceiling beam. A double wide yoga mat taking up half the living room.

Her laptop was a 2008 MacBook. I'd done some hardware upgrades on it when I got the chance. She only used it for Zoom calls, and it was usually in a bag stashed away some-where. Rarely any technology in sight. Her TV was unplugged. Used rarely. She had a bookshelf filled with books instead.

The amount of plants and how she had them everywhere. That's what got me. Not just that she had plants, but that she'd created this entire ecosystem. This living, breathing space where everything had a purpose and a place, even if that place looked like organized chaos to someone like me.

Dawn gifted me my first plant. An Aloe. I named it AL.

I went to leave one day and somehow knocked her lamp off the table.

It shattered. Glass everywhere. I felt terrible.

"I'm so sorry," I said, already trying to figure out how to clean it up, how to replace it, how to make it right.

Dawn looked at the broken lamp. Then at me.

"It's fine," she said. Completely unbothered. "I'll replace it with something greater."

Not "I'll replace it." But "something greater." Like this accident was an opportunity. Like nothing could ruin her day because she'd already decided the world was full of possibilities.

Organic chaos. Beautiful chaos. A space that felt alive.

My world was five flights of stairs with no elevator. Every trip to the car was a commitment. Parking blocks away in a parking garage.

There was no planning on my grocery runs. I knew whatever I brought I had to carry quite a ways, so I better make sure it's worth it.

Inside the studio, I had a folding table with four laptops and one screen for my desktop. IKEA furniture. Efficient. Minimal. Functional. Nothing extra. Artwork I'd painted lining the walls. Stars. Smiles. Earth. Pac man. Hearts. Most of the circles were the exact size of my kitchen dishes because that's what I'd used to trace them. Everything in its place. Everything serving a purpose.

Geometric precision. Clean lines. Order.

Not one plant.

Different worlds entirely.

But we kept catching up once a week.

She was one of the only people I saw face to face during those first few months. While everyone else was on Zoom calls and FaceTime and trying to figure out how to socialize through screens, Dawn and I still met up. Masked when we needed to be. Distanced when that made sense. But present. Actually there.

Dawn had a weekly meditation class on Zoom. Everything was on Zoom. Originally I was on Zoom while she was in her class. My pole classes had moved to Zoom too, which was an experience.

Trying to do pole dance from a video without an instructor present to spot you or correct your form or tell you when you're about to do something dangerous. Learning inverts and spins from a laptop screen. No one to catch you if you fell. No one to tell you your grip was wrong before you committed to a move. The camera angle never showed what you actually needed to see. You'd pause the video, try the move, realize you had no idea if you were doing it right, and either risk it or give up. It was too hard to do alone over Zoom. Too isolating. Too risky.

I dropped out after a few weeks. Started doing meditation with Dawn instead. We'd sit in her living room with the plants and the googly eyed fridge and breathe. Let the silence settle. Let the chaos of the world outside stay outside for a little while.

Dawn wrote a Pandemic Poem in 2020. It captured every-thing we were feeling. The isolation. The fear. The strange new world we were living in. The choice to find light anyway.

We hung out more and more as the weeks turned into months. Lot of laughs together. Lot of good times. The world was falling apart outside but inside her plant filled condo or my geometric studio, we were okay.

3-18:
THE RIPPLE EFFECT
(2020-2023)

B ut it wouldn't have been what it was.

Until we were isolated from the rest of the world, we both had to dig in and become the people we'd been talking about becoming. The people we wanted to be but hadn't quite figured out how to be yet.

Before lockdown, I'd walked my city with a bundle of sage. The farmers market was a place I went most weeks, and I often dressed up in a bright outfit when the world felt grim.

That's when I had the idea.

March 2020. As soon as lockdown started. I was going stir crazy in my studio. Working from home. Four laptops on my folding table. Blue light burning into my retinas. The same four walls every single day.

I needed something. Some way to feel human again. Some way to create joy in a world that felt joyless.

I put a call out to friends who liked to costume. Anyone who wanted to dress up and spread some joy. Meet me at the farmers market on Saturday at 11 a.m. In costume. No plan beyond that. Show up and see what happens.

I arrived in an 80s suit with a neon hat. The suit was cream colored with a wild pattern. The hat was safety cone orange. I walked from my apartment thinking I was the only character there. Thinking I'd be standing alone like an idiot in a costume while everyone else shopped for vegetables in normal clothes.

One of the vendors spotted me. Called out from behind her table.

"You need to go around the corner and meet the character in the plague mask."

I walked around the corner.

Dawn was the only one who had shown up.

She was wearing a plague mask she'd made herself. Black fabric. Long bird-like beak. The kind of mask doctors wore during the Black Death in medieval Europe. Both historically appropriate and perfectly pandemic themed.

We looked at each other. Started laughing.

For that first adventure, we kept it simple. Just walked the market. Said hello to vendors. Waved at people. Answered questions about our costumes. Had conversations with strangers who were also starved for human connection.

Pandemic time was when everyone talked to everyone. Because we were all inside so much. All isolated. All desperate for any kind of interaction that wasn't through a screen.

People stopped us constantly. Asked about the masks. Asked where we got them. Asked if they could take photos. We said yes to everything. Made people smile. Made people laugh. Gave them something weird and wonderful in the middle of all the fear and uncertainty.

What started as a one-time thing became weekly costume adventures.

At first, we'd just say "See you at 11" before parting ways. No theme. No coordination. Show up next Saturday and see what happens.

Week two was Batman and Mad Max. I wore my bright blue suit covered in repeating yellow Batman logos. Dawn had brown leather shoulder armor and tall brown feathers extending from her hair like some post-apocalyptic warrior crown. The contrast was perfect. Superhero meets wasteland survivor.

Week three was Waldo and Carmen Sandiego. A crowd pleaser from the beginning.

Week four we dressed formal.

Week five, we started coordinating themes. Before we parted ways that Saturday, we agreed on French for next week. That was it. No communication after that. No text. No Facebook messages. Nothing. We'd each go create whatever "French" meant to us, and then find out Saturday what the other one had made.

I showed up in my mime outfit. Black and white striped shirt. White gloves. Face paint.

Dawn was in a beautiful red dress with a beret.

We both started laughing when we saw each other. The berets. Tilted at the exact same angle. We hadn't planned it. Hadn't coordinated beyond the word "French." Both independently decided that's what it meant.

The market caught on.

Week after week, they'd watch us find each other. Watch our reactions to each other's costumes. It became part of the fun for them. Some of the vendors said this was the most exciting part of their week. They had to see what was going to happen right in front of them.

And none of us could predict it. Not me. Not Dawn. None of us. Because none of us knew what the other was wearing until we showed up.

Our costumes started to sync up without us communicating between Saturdays. It was comical for people to watch. We'd agree on "pirates" or "neons" or "crazy hats" before parting, and then independently create something, and somehow we'd match. Colors coordinated. Themes aligned. Energy perfectly balanced.

The market itself was a 1927 brick building with concrete floors. Indoor market hall with vendor stalls set up throughout. High ceilings strung with lights. The kind of place that had housed farmers selling their own produce for decades. A strict "farmer must grow" rule that had held since the beginning.

When we were in costume mode, we were performers. Part of the market. Part of the community.

We did this three to four weekends a month for three to four years. The costumes evolved.

Week three had been Waldo and Carmen Sandiego on shoes. A crowd pleaser from the beginning. A few months later, we brought them back on roller skates. Now we were doing it in costume through ghost town streets.

The streets were empty. Everyone was home. The whole world had shut down and here we were, two people in costumes rolling through it.

As the weeks progressed, we went further. Into the neighborhoods. Eventually covering as much of town as possible. We'd skate until it started to get dark, then head back.

We started seeing the jokes. Written on windows. Kids' handwriting. Markers and paint. Messages left for whoever might pass by during lockdown.

"*Q: Why did the bicycle fall over?*"

We'd slow down to read the answer written below.

"*A: It was two-tired.*"

Dawn and I would look at each other through our masks and laugh. Roll on to the next street.

"*Q: How do you make a tissue dance?*"

"*A: You put a little boogie in it.*"

Sometimes we'd see the kids in the windows watching us. We'd wave. They'd wave back.

The jokes stayed up for weeks. We'd pass the same houses and see new ones added. A running conversation through windows between kids who were bored and two adults on skates who were trying to spread some weird joy.

I was in full mime character one Saturday. White face paint, black lines around my eyes and mouth, the traditional look. Black and white striped shirt, white gloves, the works. Dawn was with me in her red dress.

Outside on the sidewalk near a coffee shop, a woman stopped me.

Absolutely geeked. Her whole face lit up.

"Oh my god, a mime!" she said. "A real mime! I've never seen one in person!"

I kept the act going. Gestured to my mouth, shook my head, mimed being trapped behind an invisible wall. The classic moves.

She was bouncing on her feet, genuinely delighted. "This is amazing. Can I take a picture?"

I nodded, struck a pose. She pulled out her phone.

Then she asked something else about the face paint. What kind I used, where I got it.

And without thinking, I answered her.

Out loud.

"Oh, it's just regular—"

I stopped mid-sentence.

We both froze.

Then we both burst out laughing. Dawn too, cracking up next to me. The mime had broken character completely. Fifteen seconds into a conversation and I'd forgotten I was supposed to be silent.

Dawn caught the whole thing on our camera. All three of us standing there on the sidewalk, cracking up.

We brought mime back later with roller skates. Made signs that said "mime in training" because we knew we'd mess it up, but that was half the fun. Rolling through the market in silence. Interacting with invisible walls. Pulling invisible ropes. Trapped in invisible boxes. The whole bit.

Not everything went smoothly on skates.

The same state park where I'd had my bike accident years before. We were skating this time, rolling through the paths in costume. I fell just past where the bike accident had happened. Some cosmic joke about that location and me hitting the ground.

But this time I was wearing my derby pads.

Fell at 12mph according to the camera. Just plastic scraping as I slid forty feet across the pavement, laughing so loud the whole way down. The sound of protective gear doing exactly what it was designed to do.

I can only imagine how bad it would have been without that gear. The pads were worth every penny. Still are. No injury. Not even a bruise.

It's on video. Dawn had to keep going and not look back. Couldn't stop on skates without losing momentum. Had to hold her own until she could circle back and come help me up.

Both of us laughing by the time she got back to me.

After the mime was so loved, we decided to coordinate being mimes together. That's when things started to shift. We began meeting at my place because I was closer to the market. Dressing up together. Coordinating our costumes a little better.

I don't remember what week that happened. Don't remember when it shifted. It happened so naturally, without effort. Neither of us could tell you the exact moment.

I moved apartments in June 2021. Studio to loft with a pool. The landlord kept the pool open during the pandemic. Way more space. Bed upstairs, comfortable couch downstairs. Dawn helped me move. We weren't seeing other people during the pandemic, so it made sense.

The new space changed things. More room to spread out. More room to stay.

That's when things shifted even more between Dawn and me. Where we would coordinate more. Communicate more. That's when we really knew it was a thing. Because it had been over a year of doing costumes and we were still coming up with more and more ideas.

August 2021 was Dream Cruise. A huge car cruise that's twenty miles long. Classic cars bumper to bumper.

I was a bee with a stinger. I'd brought a yellow shirt and painted the stripes on it.

Dawn was the beekeeper.

We decided to chase each other down the sidewalk nearby. Playing. Having fun. The heat was brutal but we kept going.

When we got six miles away, we realized we'd gone too far. The heat. The exhaustion. We had to call an Uber to go home.

After the first year, we started doing stilts. 2022. We had to practice before we could take them out in public. Handcrafted peg stilts built by an aerial and circus school in Ohio. Dense, solid wood adding twenty-four inches of height. To secure them, we wrapped heavy-duty nylon webbing around our calves and shins, pulling the buckles until the blood flow slowed slightly. There could be zero give. The wood had to become a literal extension of our legs. Thick rubber stoppers capped at the bottom. The size of a racquetball, smelling like burnt tires. Our only connection to the earth.

We did stilts together. Always together.

One day we wore our most outrageous pants on stilts. I was in orange neon. Dawn was in green neon. My pants were glitter silver. Hers were black and white stripes.

The glitter pants got me at Main and 4th.

I was crossing the street and I'd forgotten to safety pin the pants properly. With costumes on stilts you have to plan for all the variables. Loose fabric catching on the wooden poles, wind catching wide sleeves, weight distribution shifting everything. I'd missed one step.

The glitter fabric caught on my legs mid-step.

Went down hard. Not injured, just embarrassed and tangled in my own costume at a downtown intersection. Once I was okay, there was laughter. Safety pins next time.

We brought Waldo and Carmen back a few months later. On stilts this time. Third version of that costume. Always making little modifications to them.

The market vendors were inside the building, tables on each side of the big center aisle loaded with vegetables and baked goods and crafts. People moved around us, shopping, chatting, pointing at our height.

A kid noticed one day. Maybe four or five years old. Mobile, curious about everything, but staying close to mom and dad.

The kid stared up at Dawn. Way up. Tilted their head back to see her face.

"How did you grow such long legs?"

Pure curiosity. No filter. The way kids ask questions.

Dawn smiled down at them. "It's okay," she said, and I watched her shift her weight, move in a way that revealed what she was standing on.

The kid's eyes went wide.

"It's made of wood," one of the parents said, leaning in to point.

Absolute delight spread across the kid's face. Understanding. Joy. The kind of joy that only happens when something impossible becomes possible right in front of you. When magic gets explained and somehow becomes more magical.

And I saw it spread. The ripples. Parents smiling at each other. Other shoppers pausing to watch the exchange. Vendors at their tables grinning. This one moment of a kid learning how stilts work, creating this wave of shared delight that moved through the whole market.

A vendor who took our picture every week became part of the ritual. We'd buy their nut butters, sometimes cookies and salsa. First stop every Saturday. Get our groceries, pose for the photo. Document this week's absurdity for the record.

Over three years, she captured everything with her phone. The progression of costumes. The evolution of our partnership. I still talk to them every time I go to the market.

We met other people. Parents who introduced us to their teenager working the family's vegetable booth. "Our daughter wanted to ask you some questions," the mom said. "About how you got started and stuff like that."

We talked about costumes, about starting small, about how weird is another way of being yourself.

Over the years we saw them change. Not dramatic. Just gradual. The way confidence builds when you're figuring yourself out. Moving from the back of the booth to the front. From organizing to interacting with customers. Radiating the kind of confidence that comes from finding yourself.

I recognized it. That progression. I'd been that shy kid once. Watching them grow into themselves felt like watching a younger version of me discover that being weird was actually okay.

The market became our community. Vendors who waited for us. Restaurant staff who'd cheer through windows when we walked past.

The bookshop owner a few blocks away who'd play piano for us when we stopped in. Give us his CDs. I have a stack of them now, cherish every one. His music makes you happy. That simple, that effective.

The high-end clothing store guy who knew so much about fashion and quality. Super classy. The kind of place where a pair of socks runs over forty dollars. We'd stop in and talk. About life, about business, about whatever was happening in the world. Say hello. No pressure to buy anything. Genuine connection.

We had a whole circuit of shops we'd hit. The ones who were happy to see us became regulars. We kept coming back.

We saw so much kindness from the vendors. People who'd lived full lives and had stories if you took the time to listen. People who made space for weird in the middle of everything falling apart.

As it continued through summer and fall, the costumes got more elaborate.

The food vendors became part of our ritual. Every Saturday, 11am, they'd start looking around for us. We talked to everyone. Good banter. They'd comment on whatever ridiculous outfit we were wearing that week.

The honey pecan cluster vendor was a big bald guy with a great beard. Always wore a honey bee shirt. Always a tee shirt. He had such a love of bees. Managed his own hives plus a few others in various communities around town.

First time Dawn and I tried his pecan honey clusters, we both looked at each other mid-bite.

"These are incredible," Dawn said.

"Too incredible," I said. "What's in these?"

We were so high on life, so geeked about how good they tasted, that we actually texted him in a panic later that day.

"Are there drugs in your honey?"

He laughed. Texted back: "There are no drugs in my honey. You are just experiencing honey made with love."

That became a running joke. Every week we'd come back for more "drugs." He'd give us great hugs. Tell us about his bees. About which flowers they were visiting that season. About how the honey tasted different depending on what was blooming.

The pierogi vendor sold them in sets of three. Each one the size of a muffin. I almost always got sweet cheese and kraut. Dipped mine in sour cream. Dawn dipped hers in applesauce. We tried all the flavors over the years, but those were our go-tos.

Thinking about them makes my mouth water.

The sweet potato pie vendor had started their booth to make some extra money. It had so much fun it became how they made most of their money. Once people tasted them, you needed more. The right balance of crust to sweet potato filling.

We always talked to them but didn't always buy from them. Some weeks we'd be traveling, so we wouldn't buy much of anything other than car foods. Some weeks the market was so busy nobody had time to talk. It got busier and busier as people adjusted to pandemic times. Maybe a head nod. Maybe we'd catch them next week.

One vendor did dog treats. The one next to them did banana bread.

Dawn and I don't have any pets, so we never bought treats. But we'd always talk to both booths. Try to avoid the banana bread because it's so good you'll eat the whole loaf. Especially when the vendor tells you to cook it like French toast.

We'd talk about life, costumes, whatever was happening in the world.

One week I was Andy Warhol. Dawn was René Magritte. The Son of Man painting. A man in a dark suit and bowler hat with a green apple floating in front of his face.

The dog treat vendor looked at us. "Okay, I get Warhol. But who are you?"

Dawn explained. The apple symbolizing hidden realities. The mystery behind appearances. Magritte's interest in the relationship between the visible and the concealed.

Both vendors got animated. Started talking about fun facts they'd learned growing up. What they remembered about each artist. It turned into a whole history lesson right there between the dog treats and the banana bread.

Eggs. Vegetables. Nut butter. Dessert. Over three years, these vendors watched us show up week after week. Different costumes, different themes, different levels of absurdity. But always the same people underneath.

With Halloween coming up, we decided to pick up a few pumpkins from the market the week before to carve and wear as heads. They were kept inside the market building because of the gang of squirrels that ran the neighborhood.

We made food first at my place. Then sat around with our pumpkins, knives, spoons, plastic sheets spread out on the floor.

"Okay," Dawn said. "We're not letting each other see until we're done."

I laughed. I knew I was up against an artist. Didn't expect to stand a chance. But I know how to do a classic pumpkin look. Triangles and squares. I've got kindergarten down.

We turned our chairs away from each other. Started cutting.

The smell hit immediately. That wet, earthy, slightly sweet pumpkin smell. Scooping out all the seeds and guts. Getting our hands sticky with pulp. Carving the eye holes big enough to actually see through.

It took hours.

We talked while we worked. About life. About how crazy the pandemic had been. About how excited this made us every week. The costumes. The market. The community. All of it.

As we got later and later into the night, we got more and more delirious. Rambling about nonsense and points of view and whatever came to mind. Laughter. Pure laughter about nothing and everything at once.

My apartment had a back porch. We could sit out there and watch people come in and out of the liquor store across the way.

We sat there with our carving tools, getting silly.

"That guy's buying wine for a first date," I said, watching someone walk out with a bottle.

"No way," Dawn said. "That's clearly an apology bottle. He forgot an anniversary."

"Or maybe he's celebrating getting fired."

"From his dream job that he hated."

We'd make up stories about what people were doing. What their lives were. Who knows if any of it was true. Probably none of it. But it was imagination. Play. Like we were kids again, imagining all the possibilities of anybody being anything.

Finally we finished carving.

"Okay," Dawn said. "Ready?"

"Ready."

We turned our chairs around.

Dawn's pumpkin was unbelievably beautiful. Intricate. Artistic. You wouldn't expect anything else from her.

Mine was kindergarten. Triangles and squares. Classic. Functional.

We both started laughing.

"They're perfect," Dawn said.

"Yours is amazing," I said.

"Yours has character," she said.

Saturday morning we wore them to the market. Heavy. Really heavy. But it was cold out, so at least we weren't over-heating. We wore knit hats underneath for head protection, face masks as required during the pandemic. The inside smelled like pumpkin, and the smell stuck in your nose.

Navigating was nearly impossible. Limited vision through the eye holes. No peripheral awareness. The weight throwing off our balance. We bumped into each other constantly. Almost collided with shoppers.

Vendors were laughing at us. The vendor who always took our pictures was doubled over laughing while trying to hold her phone steady.

We somehow made it through. An hour maybe before we called it.

Walked back carefully. Slowly. Then removed each other's pumpkin heads, laughing and gasping for fresh air.

Worth it.

The sweet potato pie vendor's daughter showed us something a few weeks later. She'd been making TikToks of us showing up every week, doing 360 spins near their booth as we talked to vendors.

We were on stilts that day. She pulled out her phone, excited. "You're on TikTok. Someone's been filming you every week."

She airdropped us the videos right there. A whole reel. Multiple weeks compiled together. Us in different costumes, different themes, walking through the market, interacting with vendors, doing our thing.

It was validation. Proof that the joy we were trying to spread was actually landing. That people weren't tolerating our weirdness. They were celebrating it enough to make it content.

As it got colder, we decided to coordinate Victorian Christmas on stilts.

We prepped at my place. Got the costumes ready, made sure everything was in order. Then out to the parking lot for the stilts.

Stilt pants first. Then the stilts themselves, strapped to our legs. Knee pads. Wrist guards. Safety equipment that would stay hidden under our outfits. We were quick. Maybe five minutes.

Then we checked each other over.

"Knee pads snug?"

"Yeah. Wrist guards?"

"Good. Safety pins closed?"

We went through the whole checklist. Made sure nothing would shift or move once we started walking. Once you're on stilts moving through a market, there's no stopping to adjust. Everything has to be right from the start.

I wore a black double-breasted coat with a tall top hat decorated with greenery and a pinecone. Wide black trousers over my stilts. Grey face mask. Long wooden cane. Peg stilts don't allow you to stand still more than a few seconds, so we needed the support. Yellow name tag visible on my coat, telling people to visit our Ripple Effect social media where we made a video of each week's experience. Battery-operated white lights sewn into the fabric, steady burn, making me look almost covered in glitter.

Dawn wore burgundy velvet over a white ruffled high-collar blouse. Black top hat with a red band and more greenery. Her own cane topped with a gold bow and pinecone. Colorful patterned mask. More white lights on her costume, matching mine.

And around her waist, the hula hoop dress she'd made from her retired hoops. An evergreen wreath about four feet wide, decorated and lush. More lights woven through the greenery.

It was cold. December cold. But we barely felt it. Too focused on the costumes, the performance, the moment.

We split up. Different doors. Plan was to meet in the middle by the nut butter booth.

I walked in through the east entrance. Concrete floor under my stilts and cane. Each step deliberate. A mechanical, percussive THUD-BUMP as the rubber hit the concrete. A low-frequency sound people felt in their chest before they looked up to see what was coming. Careful. Static balance is impossible on peg stilts. I was trapped in perpetual motion. A slow, deliberate march. Left-right-left. Knees slightly bent to absorb the shock. My balance point had migrated from my hips up to the center of my sternum.

The market was loud. Dogs barking. People talking. Vendors calling out. The sound of a hundred conversations happening at once. I couldn't hear my own costume moving, couldn't hear the tap of my cane over all that noise.

People saw me. Started smiling. Even through the masks you could see it. A smile that's big enough shows in your whole body. The way people's shoulders relax. The way they lean toward something that delights them.

Some just looked and pointed. Some pulled out phones to take pictures. Most kept shopping but with that smile, that moment of joy in the middle of their Saturday routine.

I made my way to the nut butter booth.

Dawn was already there.

Walking toward me from the west entrance. Eight feet tall on her stilts. The hula hoop dress moving with each step. She looked like a bell ringing. The whole wreath swaying and flowing with her careful movements, the greenery catching the light, the white lights making her glow like she was covered in glitter.

The vendor who always took our pictures had her phone out. Already capturing this. She was amazing at it. Showed you don't need a fancy camera to take good pictures. An eye for the moment and a willingness to document it.

People stopped shopping to watch Dawn move through the market. That impossible Victorian bell of a person bringing Christmas magic on stilts. Kids stared. Adults smiled. Someone clapped.

Dawn was loving it. You could tell. Not from her movement or her posture. From something deeper. The way she inhabited the costume. The way she made space for magic in a world that desperately needed it.

Later when I saw the pictures, that's what struck me most. How alive she looked. How present. How completely herself in that moment.

We stood together by the nut butter booth. Posed for photos. Talked to vendors. Made our way through the market one careful step at a time, our canes tapping on concrete, our lights glowing, our ridiculous Victorian Christmas selves spreading joy to anyone who'd accept it.

We even had one week where we walked the market, came out to the car to drop off our groceries, then switched costumes in the parking lot to see who would notice. She switched to Waldo and me to Carmen. We went back in for coffee and pastries. The double takes by vendors were worth it.

We met at 11am at the market each week. Didn't walk in together. We wouldn't start doing that until about a year in. But once we found each other, we walked together getting our groceries and catching up with people.

First year of the pandemic, we started trading food.

Weekly meal prep exchanges at my place. Dawn's apartment wasn't near the market, so after we finished our Saturday routine, we'd head back to mine.

It started because I don't give empty containers back. She'd bring me something in a container, I'd fill it with something I'd made and hand it back. Simple system.

I made homemade Clif bars. Mixed dates, oats, peanut butter, brown rice syrup, chocolate chips into these dense energy bars that actually tasted good. Other weeks I'd make crackers from scratch. Whatever I was experimenting with.

Dawn was a really good cook. I remember how her food tasted. That immediate reaction of wanting to eat it right then and there instead of saving it for later. Her foods often included chickpeas, and I never knew how versatile and tasty they are. This sense memory of how good it was, how much care she put into it.

The exchange became part of the ritual. Market, costumes, vendors, community, then back to my place to swap containers. Another way of taking care of each other during a time when the world felt dangerous and uncertain.

Most weeks we prepped costumes at our own homes, then met up Saturday morning to see what the other had created.

We'd have a whole week to make a costume. Everyone was working from home. Nobody was going anywhere. It felt like an obscene amount of time.

Then the night before would arrive and I'd still be up at midnight finishing.

I tried to work in stages. Get the costume done earlier in the week so I could focus on food prep the night before. I love to bake cookies. But somehow it always came down to late nights. Paint and glue. Learning to sew from Dawn. My first mask came from her teaching me, so I was still new at it.

Dawn stayed up until 2am one night making a hat out of construction paper. Mind-blowing. The commitment to craft was real.

When we prepped together, we'd get slap-happy by the end. Crazy tired but wired on creativity. I don't remember what we said. How it felt. Unfiltered and ridiculous as it got later. Being kids again. Everything was play. We had no rules. Nobody could tell us what to do.

Just create whatever came out. Whatever we finished was what we'd wear. No judgment. No pressure. Pure freedom.

Saturdays started at 11am at the market. But they didn't end there anymore.

We'd come back to my place after the market. Hang out. Talk. Make food. Work on next week's costumes. Play. Everything became play. The space we held with each other and the high we got from making others smile kept us going.

Hours would pass. Afternoon into evening into night.

We would talk on the couch together, and a few times after the energy crash we would both fall asleep there. At first Dawn would crash in the late afternoon. Then as weeks went on, it got later. Staying until dark, then later still, then midnight, then 1am. Eventually she'd fall asleep there, exhausted from a full day of creating joy and being weird together.

I miss that couch.

My places have always had an open couch for friends. Wherever I live, there's a spot if someone needs it. Not unusual. I've had a number of friends crash over because, or while they work through something. Friends are there for each other.

Three years of market Saturdays. Three years of costumes and community and food exchanges and late nights.

Dawn falling asleep on my couch. Two people who found each other in the middle of a pandemic.

3-19:
THE SUPPORTER
(2021)

One year earlier, in July 2021, I met Marcus at a drum circle at a friend's house. I didn't know what to expect. People sat in a circle and beat drums while others danced. Some talked, free of judgment, letting whatever they needed out. I was fascinated watching people create that kind of space for each other.

Marcus and I hit it off immediately and started hanging out. We'd take each other on adventures. Trusting the universe and following the energy. There wasn't much planning other than a water bottle in the cup holder and a time of arrival. The rest was made up along the way.

After doing that for a while, Marcus invited me to try a sweat lodge with him. I had some experience with Native American traditions from childhood. My uncle worked at a tribe in the

Upper Peninsula, and we went to pow wows growing up. This was a different tribe, but I had some cultural awareness. The sweat lodge was a purification ceremony. Intense, humbling, and beautiful. We went to a few together, and each time I understood a little more about what this work meant to him.

Then he asked if I would support him on his Vision Quest, a multi-day, solitary vigil in nature. It was a serious, ten-day commitment.

I was honored. Vision quest was on my list when I was younger, but I never had the guts. I said yes without hesitation.

The preparation took months and involved creating prayer offerings. Small bundles that would mark sacred space. We'd meet at each other's houses, share a meal, and work together. Small squares of colored cloth. The feel of the fabric between my fingers. The scent of the loose tobacco. Spicy and rich. Tying hundreds of them on a single, unbroken string. Each bundle was a prayer. Marcus needed help with this work, and I was honored to assist.

The support camp was on sacred land. People came from all walks of life. The identities we carried in the outside world dropped away. You were either kitchen crew, fire crew, or a supporter. That was it.

Our camp was spread across a valley. The sacred fire burned continuously for four days, tended by the fire crew around the clock. It wasn't a campfire. It was something else. The fire crew didn't just watch it. They fed it. Added wood with intention. The scent wasn't the sharp, acrid smell of a bonfire. It was layered. Sweet vanilla scent. Sharp medicinal smell. Earthy woodspice. It was more than warmth and light. It was a beacon for the questers out on the land, a constant reminder that they were held by community even in their solitude.

The sweat lodge was willow branches bent and lashed into a dome. Covered in layers of heavy canvas and wool blankets until it was light-tight. A small hill. A womb.

A snake had made its home on the roof of our sweat lodge. On multiple occasions, when I went to move the cover to prepare for the ceremony, I accidentally knocked him to the ground. I knew we were in nature, in harmony with all the beings that called this land home. I wasn't just a supporter. I was a neighbor. I would gently pick him up and place him back on the roof, apologizing quietly for the disruption.

The ceremony began on Sunday evening. All the questers gathered for final preparations before their journey into solitude. My role was to hold a symbolic connection to Marcus while he was out on the land. Simply being there, maintaining the connection, being a steady presence while he did the work only he could do.

And then Marcus was alone out there, and I was back at camp.

For the next four days, I carried that connection with me everywhere. No technology. No escapes. Nothing but me, the wind, and the time to be.

For the first twenty-four hours, the silence felt like physical pressure on my eardrums. That same dead feeling I'd experienced behind the fire-break in the paper warehouse, but bigger. After years of the constant whine of data centers, the valley felt like stepping into nothing. Eventually, my brain adjusted. The silence thinned out, and I began to hear the layers underneath. The dry rustle of a snake moving through grass. The way the wind changed pitch moving through different types of trees. The distant, rhythmic sound of the sacred fire.

The first few nights, I had vivid dreams about Marcus's brother and people I didn't know. Glimpses of a life that wasn't mine. I was extra hungry. I, who was never a midnight snacker, found myself waking up with intense food cravings. A deep, hollow ache that felt like my metabolism had been hijacked. I'd head out to the van for snacks. I had stocked it with almost anything anyone could need to run a camp. Eating for two while he was fasting. It was wild and unexplainable, but others in the camp had experienced the same thing with the questers they were supporting.

At night, we could hear fireworks randomly going off in the countryside. It was July, and people were celebrating Independence Day. The sound would echo across the valley, a reminder that the normal world was still out there. Still going about its business while we were here, doing this work.

There was also the sound that would always make me laugh. The distant, sharp slam of the porta-potty door echoing across the valley. That sharp, plastic thwack. It was a funny, human punctuation mark in the middle of all that silence. We all knew the rule. Keep the seat down to make sure the smell didn't blow over camp on still nights.

At one point, another supporter and I were sent into town for propane and water. Every single person we passed stopped to talk to us. I remember two older ladies in line who could tell we were "up to something." I played along, asking them where two guys on a mission for mischief could find a good chocolate bar. They giggled and gave us directions to a local candy shop. The connection was real, free of the usual barriers between strangers.

When the four days were over, we returned to bring the questers back to camp. The ceremony concluded, and they were able to share their experiences if they chose to. Our job as supporters was to simply be there. To feed them, walk with them, and witness their return.

The chief gave me a small, wooden cedar box at the end of camp, a gift for my service. Hand-joined wood holding a deep, reddish-gold color. When I opened it, the smell was sharp and clean. The crisp scent of cedar and forest, holding a hint of the sacred smoke that had been in everything at camp.

3-20:
BUILDING WALDO
(2021)

I bought my first van without knowing how to build one. That's how most things in my life had worked by then: figure it out as you go, learn from the mistakes, ad. The 2020 road trip had proven I could work from anywhere with three laptops and layered WiFi connections. Now I needed to build that anywhere into something more permanent than a coffin tent and a sedan.

In 2021, I found a 2007 Chevrolet Express at a government auction. A landscape of white, utilitarian fleet vehicles. Waldo sat there as a blank slate, smelling of previous work and industrial metal. White, 197k miles already on it. Fifteen hundred bucks. Maybe sixteen hundred. The kind of money where if you completely destroy it learning, you're not bankrupt.

That price tag gave us permission to be stupid.

At the farmers market, people helped me brainstorm names. "Vanna White" got a laugh. I appreciate a good pun. But "Waldo" stuck. Something about the idea of being hard to find, of disappearing into adventure, of people asking "Where's Waldo?" while I was out there living.

I sold my silver sedan. Someone offered me more than I owed on it, and the timing felt right. Waldo would be my only vehicle now. No going back. No safety net. A white cargo van with 197,000 miles and absolutely zero amenities.

Manual locks that clicked with a satisfying thunk. Manual windows that required actual physical effort to roll down. The only thing automatic was the transmission. No fancy technology. Metal and intention and the willingness to figure things out as they broke or didn't work the way I'd planned.

Dawn and I set up a rhythm. We'd discuss ideas all week long, bouncing concepts back and forth over text and phone calls, drawing things on paper, watching YouTube videos on our own time. Then one day a week, we'd head to her parents' house to work on the van in their driveway. A summer rhythm of sawdust, YouTube tutorials, and borrowed tools. The air was hot. After, we'd swim in her parents' pool and have dinner with them. The cool water after hours of working in the heat.

It was seriously one of the best ways to spend a summer.

Her dad had tools. Lots of tools. A hole saw we didn't have. Knowledge about building things that neither of us possessed. He was happy to loan us both, to be part of the build without taking over. He'd watch, offer advice when asked, crack jokes with timing so dry you'd miss it if you weren't paying attention.

The first major terror: cutting through the roof.

You can't undo that. If you screw it up, if you cut in the wrong place or at the wrong angle, I have no idea how you'd fix it. The van wasn't expensive, but still. Once you cut through metal, there's no going back.

Dawn did it while her dad watched.

She taped off her template. Measured three times. Drilled four holes in the corners. Then grabbed the jigsaw and started cutting corner to corner. The jigsaw blade screamed as it bit through the metal roof. I held my breath, terrified that one wrong angle would ruin the entire van.

Halfway through, her dad said in the most deadpan voice imaginable: "It's not going through."

Dawn froze. Stopped cutting. Started to panic.

Then she realized he was messing with her.

The man had dry humor that could stop your heart if you weren't ready for it. She finished the cut. Perfectly placed. Clean edges. The first vent hole in Waldo's roof, and we hadn't destroyed anything.

I'd been holding my breath the entire time.

We did it again for the second vent. Then for shore power. Each time, that moment of terror before the cut, wondering if this would be the one that went wrong. Each time, it worked.

Before the insulation and tapestry, the van was a hollow metal shell. Every spoken word bounced off the windows and bare walls. The echo made conversations feel weird, unfinished.

The learning curve was steep and constant.

I insulated it wrong the first time. Had to pull it all out and redo it. Made mistakes with the wiring that could have been dangerous if we hadn't caught them during testing. We did test runs constantly. Checking seals. Making sure nothing leaked. Making sure nothing would catch fire or electrocute me in my sleep.

The satisfying moments came in layers.

When we put the counter in, a repurposed kitchen island that fit perfectly, I felt something shift. It felt solid and anchored, a physical sign that the cargo hold had transformed into a living space. Not a cargo van with holes cut in the roof. An actual mobile home.

The shelving was even better. I figured out a way to mount it that gave us access to storage, created a channel for LED strip lighting behind the shelves, and housed the battery where we could get to it if needed. Channels of light hidden behind the shelving that glowed at night, turning the industrial interior into a space that felt calm and deliberate. It looked good. It functioned well. I'd solved a problem with my own brain and hands.

Dawn hung a tapestry for a ceiling. Not permanent. That was the genius of it. No drywall trapping mistakes we'd made. We could pull it back anytime something needed checking or fixing.

She talked about color theory during the build. Complimentary colors. How certain shades could make a space feel calming while others would make you want to leave. It changed how I looked at everything. Made me notice billboards designed by people who clearly had no idea what they were doing. Just because you like two colors together doesn't mean they look good to the human eye.

Her mom was an art teacher. That helped. We had knowledge transfer happening from every direction.

What fascinated me most was watching how differently we approached every single task.

Sound dampening material. We both did it. Both got great results. Completely different methods. Same with laying tile. Same with mounting anything to the walls. She'd have her way. I'd have mine. Neither was wrong. Both worked.

Dawn could freehand draw anything on a napkin. Beautiful, detailed sketches of what we were trying to build. I used computers to aid my design process, measuring three times digitally before cutting once in real life. Different brains. Same destination.

She was right about things more often than I wanted to admit.

Before I left for the cross-country trip, I had a timeline. Had to get on the road. I thought it would be brilliant to take a 9-cube storage unit, you know, those modular shelf things, and mount it in the van for organization.

Dawn was resistant. Explained why it wouldn't work. I didn't listen.

By the time she met up with me in Vegas, the thing was destroyed. Every road vibration had eaten at the structure until the unit was completely removed from the van. The structure didn't have the integrity to handle it. Everything that was supposed to stay in the cubes had shifted and traveled. I'd open the van and find my stuff scattered everywhere across the van floor. The rigid, computer-aided design process didn't account for the road-truth that the vibration of the highway doesn't care about your digital measurements.

She laughed when she saw it was gone. Didn't say "I told you so," though she absolutely could have.

I listened to her after that.

Our dynamic worked because we had no judgment about ideas. One of us would pitch something. The other would ask questions. We'd explain what we were trying to accomplish. Then we'd bounce ideas back and forth until we found a solution we both agreed on.

No ego. No "my way or the highway." two people figuring out how to build something neither of us knew how to build.

Her dad's tools were borrowed. The YouTube videos were free. Most of the materials were repurposed or salvaged or bought secondhand. We were building Waldo on a budget that proved you don't need money to change your life.

You need willingness to figure it out as you go.

By the end of summer 2021, Waldo was drivable. Not finished. Not perfect. But functional enough to test. Ready to see what would break.

The manual locks clicked with a satisfying thunk. The manual windows required actual effort to roll down. The first time I drove with the roof vents open, there was a sharp rush of road noise, a new sound that hadn't existed before we'd cut those holes. The manufacturer warned not to open them while moving or we'd break the fan. The counter held our camp stove. The shelving stored our gear. The LED strips lit up the interior at night.

It worked.

More importantly, I'd built it. Dawn and I had built it. With borrowed tools and YouTube videos and her dad's dry humor and a willingness to cut through metal even when it scared the hell out of us.

Waldo sat there in that driveway, waiting.

3-21:
WALDO'S JOURNEY
(2021-2023)

The first real test came that same year: a loop around Lake Michigan. Dawn and I loaded up and headed north through the Upper Peninsula, down through Wisconsin, back through Chicago.

I felt the vibration of the 197,000-mile engine traveling through the steering column and into the webbing of my thumbs. The steering wheel was a thin, hard-textured plastic circle that felt oversized in the narrow cab. The manual windows required a rhythmic, circular motion of the arm to operate. Heavy plastic cranks. As they rolled down, I felt the mechanical resistance of the glass sliding into the metal door frame.

Camping along the way, meeting people, and having fun.

We stayed with my cousin in Marquette and hiked Sugarloaf Mountain, a popular scenic overlook with views that made the climb worth every step.

Somewhere along the way, I'd changed the strobe light switch and tripped a fuse without noticing. Waldo had manual everything, and the clock still worked, so I had no idea anything was wrong. By the time we got to Sault Ste. Marie, we had no running lights.

A cop pulled us over, took me out of the van to show me. Then his radio crackled, something urgent, and he rushed to give me my stuff back and left in a hurry.

That blown fuse had probably saved me from electrocution when I was working on the wiring. We traveled only during the day after that, making sure we were always somewhere by dark.

When we got back to Michigan, it took the shop an hour and most of their mechanics looking at it to figure out what I'd done. They were great about it, showed me in detail what they'd found, talked through ideas and inspirations. Now when I walk into the local shop, they all want to hear stories from recent travels and show me what they're working on.

We camped near Tahquamenon Falls, then drove to Marquette and visited Lakenenland Sculpture Park.

That first night in the woods, I lay on the mattress realizing my feet were only inches from the rear doors. The absolute silence of the woods broken by the occasional creak of the van's metal cooling down in the night air. I felt the temperature difference - the warmth of my sleeping bag against the cold, uninsulated metal of the door handle. Rolling over in a space that was exactly the width of my shoulders. I developed the van-pivot - a calculated movement of the hips and knees to avoid hitting the cabinetry.

Lakenenland: over 100 metal sculptures made from scrap that you could drive through and view from your vehicle. Junkyard art: a dinosaur fishing, a band on a stage, a sculpture of a Michigan woman. The state had told them they couldn't have it, so they made it free and opened it 24/7 as a park. Rebellion through generosity.

Down into Wisconsin. The farm to table campground again, where farm dogs followed us around. Kinstone, with its standing stones and that quality of land that seemed to pay attention. Dr. Evermor's Forevertron, 50 feet high, 300 tons of scrap metal transformed into a machine designed to launch its creator into the heavens. The Bird Band, a 70 member automated orchestra made entirely from found objects. Chaos as creation in its finest form.

Chicago for deep dish pizza. After that much time in nature, the city felt like a bit much, but the pizza was worth it.

The first trip passed. Waldo worked.

The next year, 2022, I went bigger. Nearly three months on the road. Eleven thousand miles. Solo through Indiana, Illinois, Missouri, Arkansas, Kansas, Oklahoma, Texas, New Mexico, Arizona, then to Las Vegas, then to Venice Beach.

Indiana first. I camped in a casino parking lot where it was 15 degrees outside. My heating system lasted two hours per propane tank and required lots of ventilation, which meant I was constantly balancing warmth against freezing.

At night inside Waldo, the LED strips cast long shadows across the repurposed kitchen counter. A dim, amber-lit cocoon. It smelled of cedar, leftover sawdust, and the clean scent of new upholstery. The tapestry ceiling hung inches above my head, soft and thick, muting the tinny acoustics of the metal van. The MaxxAir fan hummed with a steady, white-noise whir. When I ran it on high, I could feel the air physically being pulled from the floor up past my skin, creating a constant, artificial breeze in the small space.

Not ideal, but it worked.

Illinois I didn't stop for more than gas and caffeine and food. Passing through, heading west.

Somewhere between Illinois and Missouri, the storm hit. It was loud as hell on the thin metal roof. Heavy rain pounding down.

Missouri I stayed at a horse farm with electric hookup, which meant I could run my space heater. Luxury compared to the casino parking lot.

Arkansas I didn't stop.

Kansas I stopped to take a picture and make some Wizard of Oz references. Followed a yellow brick road. You can't pass through Kansas without acknowledging Dorothy.

In Oklahoma, I stayed in a treehouse Airbnb with heat. It was cold, but the hosts said it gets super hot there in the summer. The couple who owned it had lost everything during the pandemic. They'd built this Airbnb out of construction waste from a nearby housing development. The workers were happy to assist them with supplies. It was amazing. They told me it kept them afloat until the world opened again.

In Texas, I met a guy at a bar. Fun to talk to. Seemed to know a lot about the community. We got into one of those conversations that ranged from life to travels to adventure, the kind where you lose track of time because you're genuinely connecting with someone.

At the end of the night, he'd bought everyone's food in our little group. All of our meals. All of our drinks. Real Texas hospitality.

I was back on the road the next day, and there was a billboard with his picture on it. He was one of the biggest attorneys in that area of Texas.

New Mexico opened up into a different world. In Truth or Consequences, this beautiful small town where it was hot during the day and cold at night, I found something special. The campground had two water taps. One for city water. The other was the hot spring piped directly into the spigot. But here's the catch: it had to drain to the Rio Grande, so the drain system was also open air where you could watch the water work its way back to the river.

The camp host gave me a bicycle to go see it for myself. It was marvelous.

That campground had one of those evenings where everything aligned. So many people sitting around after a while, the camp host gave me a bottle of limoncello to pass out. I used this as an excuse to talk to every single other camper and invite them to the fire that evening.

By the time we got the fire going, we had a very diverse range of people. All walks of life. All orientations. All ages. All races. Everything all mixed in around one campfire, one bonfire bringing everyone together.

People would pose a question to the group or talk about why they were traveling on the road or what they were doing, and we would talk as a group about it. It was great because everybody had something to contribute. It was such a beautiful melting pot.

I seriously spent three days with these people, 24/7 pretty much other than sleep, and we took care of each other. We showed off each other's vans and talked about ideas. We showed off the things we were proud of. We asked questions about different things. It was cool.

I seriously can't count the amount of nice people I've met. Truth or Consequences probably needs its own chapter, but for now, know that it was magic.

That kind of landscape in New Mexico, you'd drive with your jaw dropped. Not another person you can see. For miles. In any direction.

Arizona to see Nick and his family. Had a nice dinner with them, caught up, then kept moving.

Las Vegas. A hotel was cheaper than most campgrounds and it was quite hot outside. I stayed on the Strip for one eighth what it costs today. It was still restricted for the pandemic. I called Dawn from California and said I'm sending her and Jade plane tickets. Come to Vegas.

Venice Beach. I'd seen the Ocean Front Walk on Baywatch as a kid. Roller skaters gliding past street performers and the Pacific Ocean. I wanted to skate it in person.

It didn't disappoint. I rented skates and hit the boardwalk, feeling like I was inside a TV show I'd watched decades ago. Street performers. Muscle Beach. The Pacific stretching out beyond. Pure childhood nostalgia made real.

In a restaurant, I heard two women talking next to me. I don't eavesdrop but it was hard not to hear. They'd both been in the acting and entertainment industry. Both were from different states. Both talking about the business, about craft, about the pursuit of it all. In a very expensive area of California.

I gave them my information. Told them if they ever needed a place to stay in Michigan or wanted to visit the Midwest, I'd host them. Real offer. Not pleasantries.

I went outside, called Dawn and said hey, would you and Jade want to go to Vegas? That's how that came about. She knew I'd been traveling awhile and could probably use some friendly company.

They flew in. I picked them up at the airport.

I'd already gone to the parking garage at the airport, which is narrow. I went in through the exit which has clearance warnings. Missed my first turn and got lost in the garage. On the way out, I caught the strobe light on the roof against a low hanging beam, and it got torn off Waldo. I had to go back later and retrieve it, along with paying for a parking ticket because I'd lost track of where I parked and how long I'd been there. That's how Tom works sometimes.

The Strip was chaos. Vegas had gone from masks and restrictions to no more masks and restrictions. There was a ton going on. Tons of people everywhere. They were a little overwhelmed. I took them a less busy way through some back hallways and got us to the room.

We saw Cirque shows. O at the Bellagio blew my mind. That stage transforms from solid floor to deep pool in seconds. As someone who does aerial, I couldn't stop thinking about what it would be like to perform over water. Your grip changes when things are damp. There's no net, no matting. Water. The high divers hitting precise marks with other performers below them. Fire elements around all that water. It looked effortless, but I knew how hard it was. That's what made it beautiful.

We explored the Strip. Caught up on life over food. Dabbled at slot machines.

These two were the people I was with during the pandemic. We spent a lot of time together when the world felt uncertain. The three of us clicked. The chemistry was undeniable. We could be completely ourselves without any performance, any holding back.

Jade is fierce. A woman so radiant she could change an entire city by setting foot in it. When I first met her at the float center, I struggled to talk to her. It was so unusual that she later told other people, "I think he hates me," because I was so quiet around her. But it wasn't hate. It was awe.

Once I got to know her, I saw the woman behind the radiance. She's witty and stoic in ways that don't usually go together. When you bring her something, anything, she never judges. She might ask a few questions, but she's not trying to fix you or solve your problem. She asks what you already know. What you're avoiding saying out loud.

That's invaluable.

Dawn does the same but differently. Both of them stay sharp, stay focused, perform at levels most people don't reach. My chaos and adventure energy balanced perfectly with their calm and clarity.

All three of us have our own way of doing things. When we come together, it works because none of us tries to change the others.

After taking Jade to the airport, Dawn and I drove on. My cousin is in Utah. He lives in a great state for adventure. Four national parks within an hour's drive of his house. We stayed with him, and he gave us tours, showed us all kinds of different things around the desert.

Zion is seriously one of my favorite places on earth. Dawn and I hiked the Narrows on this trip. It was snowing, but in Michigan that kind of snow was nothing. There were only a handful of people because of the weather. We enjoyed the beauty of it all. We got to explore the park and get some cool pictures because the snow didn't stop us at all.

Bryce was about the same. Very few people there. A lot of areas were closed due to road conditions. We had to be careful because it's snowing and you don't want to go off a cliff by sliding. But we made it work.

We accidentally found Arches on the way home and explored that park for a day. Over 2,000 natural arches carved by wind and time. Deep red and orange rock that doesn't look real. Delicate Arch standing there like it shouldn't be possible. We walked through it in awe, trying to comprehend the scale and the time it took to create something like that.

Best Friends Animal Sanctuary was one of those places. I'd seen Dogtown years ago on TV and thought I was going to go out there. Then my mom said I had a cousin who goes there, and we got in touch.

We didn't get to volunteer because it was pandemic times and they weren't taking volunteers. We were able to meet some animals and do a walking tour type thing. My cousin helped give us a drive by tour and we got to see some interesting things. There was an area you could rent for weddings that was part cave, part open desert, with water and grass in this unexpected place. He took us in his Jeep on back roads, showed us all kinds of different things.

In Colorado, I stopped to visit Chloe again. She'd settled in since my last visit, given her life a real shake up, and was thriving. Over good food, she told me she could see differences in me since she'd last seen me. It was cool to hear, having someone who knew the before version witness the after.

But I could see the differences in her too. She's one of those people that gets it. I don't even know what it is, but it's ease. We catch up and it's like we saw each other last week, even though it might have been a year or two. She's completely different. I'm completely different every time we see each other. It's so cool to have that kind of validation and see it in others too.

In Iowa, we stopped at Fong's for Asian fusion pizza. Crab rangoon and General Tso's chicken on a crust. The kind of inventive chaos that makes you laugh while you eat.

We crossed into Michigan with the fuel light on for the first time. I rarely let it get that low, but we'd lost track of time and space.

The tires hit the metal expansion joints at the bridge - a rhythmic badump-badump that vibrated through the entire chassis. The green-and-white sign passing in a blur. I checked the odometer and watched the numbers roll over, a physical tally of the distance covered. A deep, involuntary exhale. I gripped the wheel at ten and two, feeling the muscles in my forearms tighten. The sudden lightness of knowing everything I owned was currently traveling at 70 miles per hour with me.

Late night gas station, most of the lights broken and flashing. Harsh, flickering overhead fluorescent lights that made

Waldo's white paint glow. The air was thick with the smell of gasoline and hot asphalt, a sharp contrast to the quiet cabin. The place was sketchy, but we knew we were safe. Got gas, used the restrooms, made it home.

That fall, I bought a used car. Waldo was amazing for adventures and fit in regular parking spots fine. But I wanted 4x4 for Michigan winters. Passenger room for when I wasn't solo. Heated seats. Something practical for everyday life that got better gas mileage for running errands. No car payments on either one.

I sold Waldo in early 2023. Thirty thousand miles. Three years. Worth every one.

3-22:
THE SECOND BUILD
(2023-2025)

By late 2023, I was back on government auction sites. I'd sold Waldo earlier that year for exactly what I'd paid for him. Thirty thousand miles. Three years. I was still at the compound then, still walking floors and talking to people. Still thriving. The van was a weekend project, a next chapter I was building in the driveway while the current chapter kept paying the bills.

Instead, I was scrolling through listings.

I found one at a zoo. 2008 Chevrolet Express. One year newer than Waldo. 124,000 miles. The listing photos showed it parked between maintenance buildings. It turned out it was the aquarium dive team van. They'd averaged twelve hundred miles a year during its service. Where Waldo had been a city work van that knew every street in its city, this one hadn't seen the world yet.

I placed a bid and waited to see if I won it.

I did.

This one was quieter. Just as rusty. Better headlights, which mattered more than I'd realized until I had them. The rear windows didn't open, less ventilation than Waldo. Trade-offs everywhere.

I didn't name it right away. With Waldo, the name had come naturally after Dawn and I had been working on it for a while. This one would get its name when it was ready. Forcing it felt wrong.

Building the second van was different from day one. With Waldo, everything was new. Every cut was terrifying. Every decision felt permanent. Dawn and I had taped that template to the roof, drilled four corner holes, and held our breath as the jigsaw cut through metal. We didn't know if we were ruining it.

This time, I knew. I knew that cutting the roof wouldn't destroy the van. I knew that the first insulation job would be terrible and I'd redo it. I knew that the wiring would need testing and retesting. I knew that things would fall apart on the road and I'd have to fix them or live with them or completely rebuild them.

That knowledge changed everything. I still cut carefully. Still measured twice. But the terror was gone, replaced by something steadier. Confidence earned through failure.

First: destroy the past. I used a crowbar to rip out work I'd done years ago. The crunch of wood splitting. The sudden pop of screws losing their grip. There was a heavy, conflicted feeling in my chest - regret for the time spent mixed with sharp, clean relief that the old mistakes were finally being cleared out. Dust motes danced in the sunlight pouring through the open side door, highlighting the bare, scarred metal where the cabinets used to be.

Then I found the rot. Peeled back the old flooring to find damp, dark patches of wood underneath. The wood was soft, almost spongy, giving way under the pressure of a flat-head screwdriver. A sudden, sharp scent of damp earth and stagnant water - the smell of the road catching up to the vehicle. The sturdiness I thought I'd built was an illusion.

I spent hours on my hands and knees, eye-level with the wheel wells. The driveway was a construction zone - the sound of saws and the smell of sawdust. The Michigan air shifting from the heat of the day cooling into damp evening. The driveway was littered with the guts of the van: scraps of old insulation, jagged pieces of wood, ghosts of the first build. My joints ached from the hard metal surface. My shins mapped with small bruises. I could see the topography of the van floor - the ridges, the valleys, the tiny spots of surface rust that needed treatment. A slow, intimate study of the machine's foundation.

The oscillating multi-tool made a high-pitched, frantic bzzzz. When I pressed it into the van's plywood subfloor, the vibration traveled through my wrists and into my elbows. A surgical tool for a blunt job - cutting out sections of floor that had become soft and rotted over time.

The shop-vac screamed as it sucked up the debris. The hose was ribbed and stiff, making a whirring sound. It smelled of stale dust, old wood, and the ozone of a motor working overtime.

Without the cabinets or gear, the interior was a hollow, white metal cave. Cold and resonant. Every movement I made

- every knee that hit the metal floor - amplified into a loud, metallic bang that echoed in the small space.

I built different layouts, applied what I'd learned. The counter was different. Everything inside was different. The only thing that stayed the same was the wall paneling because it was cheap and effective. The flooring was thicker and insulated this time. The storage changed completely. The 9-cube organizers Dawn had warned me about? Gone. She'd been right about those. They'd fallen apart within weeks on the road. This time: real shelving. Secured properly. Built to handle movement.

The electrical system got an upgrade. I understood batteries now, understood draw and capacity in ways I hadn't before. The solar panel had five times the power of Waldo's and was the same physical size but cost half as much. It's wild how much technology changed in just a few years. LED strips everywhere I needed light. Switches that made sense. No more reaching into dark corners trying to find a connection.

Sound dampening went in better. Heavy, adhesive-backed sheets of Kilmat - butyl rubber with a silver foil face. They felt cold and dense. When I slapped them onto the bare metal walls, the tinny echo of the van's shell was replaced by a solid, muted thud. The edges were sharp - one careless slide of a finger resulted in a clean, paper-cut-style slice from the foil.

The subfloor was a layer of foam board insulation stuck to the metal, then the plywood on top. I used construction adhesive - a thick, viscous liquid that smelled of strong chemicals. It required a steady, squeezing pressure on the caulking gun. I felt the resistance in my forearm as the bead of glue slowly snaked out. I had to step carefully to avoid shifting anything before it set.

Then came the first new plywood. The slap of a large, heavy sheet of 3/4-inch plywood as it settled into place. A solid, grounding sound that signaled the end of the destruction phase. Walking across the new floor for the first time. It didn't creak. It didn't give. It felt permanent. I felt the stability in my ankles - a level, flat surface that could finally support the next version of my life.

Insulation fit tighter. I knew where the gaps would be and how to prevent them.

But I also knew something else: it didn't need to be perfect before I used it.

Dawn and I took the van east into Canada in early 2024. We crossed the border, continued east, then turned north. A few hours north of Toronto was our end target. Nine hundred miles round trip. We were tourist exploring Canada, revisiting places I'd gone to years ago combined with a few new stops along the way. It was also a test run for some of the van's parts and a great way to figure out what we required.

First stop: Niagara Falls. We stayed at a church that rented a campsite. Nobody else was there. We didn't expect mosquitos but they ran the place. We explored a little bit and relied on the power of the vent fan to suck them all to the screen and away from us.

In the morning we went to the falls to make tea and breakfast. We ate watching the falls before all the tourists arrived. It's like the Vegas of Canada.

At one point we went to a Canadian Tire. Dawn asked why we didn't need tires. "You don't understand what this place is," I said. It wasn't a tire shop. It was everything. Camping gear next to kitchen gadgets next to actual tires. The name makes no sense until you walk in and realize it's just Canada being Canada.

From there we drove to Toronto for lunch, then headed to raw public land in Canada. Free-range camping where you can stay for up to two weeks, no questions asked, no amenities. It was the first night actually sleeping in the van and it was a success. Tim Hortons in the morning, which in Canada tastes even better.

We made our way toward Algonquin Provincial Park. I figured we'd get there and find our way from there. We didn't. It started to storm. Dawn was able to get on the phone and find us a campground forty-five minutes from where we were. We got there and checked in. It was so quiet even with hundreds of campers around us, all kinds of languages, especially Canadian French more than English.

The water was crystal clear. The lake was massive, maybe four homes on the entire thing, the rest was raw land. We had showers and toilets and everything was great. We hiked, cooked, explored the campground. It's always fun to go grocery shopping in another country. Canada puts their milk in bags. It's wild.

We went to bed for the night and the door wouldn't close. Neither of us could get it to close. SLAM. SLAM. SLAM. I kept trying and decided to stop so as not to annoy other campers. Used a bungee cord to hold it shut for the night. The next morning, after using a screwdriver, tapping on a stuck pin, the door closed easily.

I took Dawn to a fire tower as a tourist attraction, and we explored the gardens.

We stayed at one more campground on the way home. At every campground, we'd gotten to know the campers around us. By Halloween there would be snow in Canada, so people were doing trick-or-treating early. Every camper told us their favorite candy bar and we collected them. Twenty-six candy bars by the time we left.

At this last campground, there was a guy who kept doing finger guns at me. I'd finger gun back. This went on for a while. He never said anything, just the finger guns and gestures. I thought he was very French. Dawn finally pointed out he was deaf and had been signing at me the whole time. I was naive. The banter was still great.

The bridge crossing back to the US took almost three hours due to construction. By the time we got to customs, I was exhausted. The customs officer asked if we had anything to declare.

"Twenty-six candy bars," I said, straight up. "We were camping and every camper told us their favorite candy bar and we did trick-or-treating because by Halloween there would be snow."

The customs officer looked at me, looked at Dawn, looked back at me. Paused. Then waved us through.

Later that spring, Jade and I took the van to Mississippi. We had friends down there we wanted to see. Nineteen hundred miles round trip.

When Jade took over driving, I had no idea where we were going. In the time she drove, we went to a crystal store, an ice cream shop, and a chocolate outlet. We had so many snacks. A giant Valentine's heart of chocolates was three dollars. We both got our chocolate fix.

We got a hotel halfway and the next morning Jade took me to see the Dambo Trolls in Kentucky. I'd never heard of them. Giant sculptures made from recycled materials, hidden in the forest. A family of three trolls. There was a trail that took us to each one. They were fascinating. Apparently they're all over the world now.

The place was awesome. They grew most of their own food and it was tasty. We met so many people and loved hearing their stories. Once we left there we made a run for home. It was worth the pitstop.

What I didn't expect was how much I'd enjoy watching someone else drive my van. Jade knows vehicles. She's comfortable behind the wheel of anything, understands weight and momentum and how to handle something that size. She wasn't treating it like my van. She was driving.

The friends we visited put us in an outbuilding with AC and water. It was hot there, but we were able to read before being kidnapped by our friends and shown the local town and a coffee shop.

One day we went on the river. Two friends with inflatable kayaks, two friends with hard plastic kayaks, and me with my inflatable stand up paddle board. It was eight hours or so on the river with a variety of conditions, no signs, rain and storms, but we kept going.

My rudder would hit a log and I would fall forward and laugh. At first I noticed I was alone, nobody else in sight. The paddle board is faster. I heard a splash and froze.

It's a gator. What do I do? It's a gator. What do I do? Oh shit.

I took a breath and turned around.

It was a beaver. I swear it was laughing at me. It scared me good.

I got ahead of the group and met them at a Y in the river with no idea where to go next. Pretty remote forest in all directions most of this ride. Then we stuck together and had a great time.

We met many great people on the property they live on, from all walks of life, all there living a simpler life for their own reasons. It was quite magical in itself.

The drive back north was long. We split the driving.

In mid-2024, Labor Day weekend, I was invited to meet some friends at a ranch a few hours outside San Antonio. Three thousand miles round trip, fifteen hundred each way. By then the operations transfer had already started eating me alive. The hives were spreading. The insomnia was getting worse. But the van was ready, and I needed to be somewhere else. I thought I'd sleep in the van the whole time.

Then I got to Texas in summer. Ninety-five degrees. Every day.

The van became an oven by noon. I couldn't sleep at night. The temperature barely dropped. I got an Airbnb. It felt like failure at first. Like I'd built this whole thing and couldn't even use it for its main purpose.

It was hot, but I got on horses early in the morning. It was a really good time.

The drive down had been fine. I'd parked in lots overnight, slept reasonably well. But I'd made one mistake that stuck with me.

One night, I was tired. My body said keep driving, find somewhere better. But I stopped at a Walmart because it was convenient and I wanted to sleep.

A semi-truck pulled in next to me an hour later. Engine running. Diesel fumes flooding into my van sucked through my fan and into the van.

I woke up coughing. I was breathing diesel all night.

Now I'm picky about where I park and sleep.

The van sits in my driveway right now as I write this. Unfinished. The badge came off three months ago. The savings are draining. There are things I want to add. Better ventilation. Solar panels. A second battery. Countertop improvements. Storage refinements.

I could wait until it's perfect. I could plan every detail, buy every part, complete every upgrade before taking it anywhere.

But waiting for perfect means missing the adventure.

I've already driven this van to Canada. To Mississippi. To Texas. It's been to eight states in various stages of completion. Sometimes the bed setup was temporary. Sometimes the electrical system was held together with zip ties. Sometimes I had to adapt on the fly.

And it worked. Not perfectly. But it worked.

3-23:
THE LAST BOX
(2019-2025)

I landed the server infrastructure job back in February 2019. I genuinely loved working there.

The laptops they gave me were high-end. Everything about that job was high-end. My days were spent walking the building, talking to people at every level. I helped build employee resource groups. I worked with teams on community events: food banks, Habitat for Humanity, being part of the world around us. My team would walk the company's nature trail almost every day. I'd think while I walked, solve problems while I moved. I had a BOSU ball at my desk. A half-sphere balance trainer, platform on top of a ball you stand on. Sitting still has never been easy for me. The BOSU ball let me keep moving while I worked.

Everything about that first team matched how I worked: prevention over reaction, solutions over monitoring, moving and talking instead of sitting and watching. I thrived there.

Those first five years were some of the best of my career.

In May 2024, I transferred to an Operations team. I thought it would be growth.

It became something else entirely.

The new role was in a different building. Connected to the main facility but isolated from it. No windows. Limited access. The people I'd built relationships with for five years were unreachable. The high-end laptops were gone, replaced with basic company computers.

The team was smart. They fit their jobs well. But their way of working wasn't my way of working. They watched screens and monitored systems. I walked floors and talked to people. Neither approach is wrong. They're different.

I couldn't adapt. The autonomy I'd had for five years was gone. I had to account for my time in ways I never had before. Some coworkers reported me to my boss for not being at my desk enough. That wasn't how I worked.

The stress began to manifest physically within weeks.

Hives covering my arms and chest. Stress-induced. My body's error log. I wore long sleeves to cover them up. They itched like hell. Constant burning itch I couldn't scratch in meetings. When I went to work, they would turn beet red. Angry welts under the fabric.

My body missed the outside. I started to struggle to know what time of year it was or what the weather was like. The natural rhythms I'd always relied on were gone.

The insomnia got worse and worse. I'd lie awake staring at the ceiling, my mind racing through everything I'd done wrong that day, every way I'd failed to fit into a box I couldn't understand.

Often I would call in sick because I didn't sleep. I couldn't function without sleep.

My entire world had fallen apart. I lost aerial arts because work was affecting me so much. The thing that had saved me. Strength and trust and facing my fear. Gone. Because I couldn't function anymore.

I took it all so seriously. At the end of the day, it was a job. There are other jobs out there. There are other ways to make money.

But I couldn't see that yet.

Some of my coworkers reported me to my boss for not being at my desk enough. That wasn't how I worked. I talked to people, walked the building, knew what was happening. I couldn't handle a job where I just looked at screens all day. That's not how I operated.

In February 2025, I went to Europe for two and a half weeks. I came back in early March.

I felt so alive. So big. So free.

I only wish I'd gone longer.

The contrast was brutal. In Europe, I'd felt like myself again. Walking foreign streets, meeting strangers, exploring without agenda. The hives had started to fade.

Then I walked back into that windowless building, back to my desk, back to the screens and the coordination and the feeling that I was doing everything wrong.

I drafted my two-week notice in March. Held onto it, thinking I could still make it work. The hives. The insomnia. The panic attacks thinking about going to work.

The breaking point came over an email.

I answered it. My boss called me, upset I'd answered without checking with him first. I didn't know I had to be micromanaged to that point.

That's when I knew.

I couldn't do it anymore.

The final weeks were a blur of mounting tension. Small conflicts that felt disproportionately large. Communication breakdowns that left me confused.

I burned through so many sick days those last few weeks. I couldn't sleep, couldn't function. When I finally handed in my notice, I still sacrificed a week of sick time I'd earned. I needed out.

In early April, I handed in my notice. April 2nd. Not April 1st, because that would look like a joke.

The exit was quick. Standard procedure. I wasn't able to say goodbye to anyone.

I walked out before I knew what was happening.

Confusion and freedom. Something that felt so real, that job was doing good for the world, was now gone and I was removed like it never happened.

Once I left, coworkers from my old team reached out. They checked on me. They made sure I was okay.

I left because staying would have broken me completely.

The badge came off in April.

Twenty years. A rectangular piece of plastic with a photo of a younger version of me. The lanyard had been around my neck so long I'd stopped feeling it. When I took it off, the weight was gone. The ghost-weight of twenty years of being on call.

I handed it in. Walked out.

The silence that followed was absolute. No pager. No alerts. No rhythmic electronic screaming of a black hole event.

Just silence.

I walk to the van. Different gait. No threat assessment scan. My shoulders are down.

The manual window crank is a heavy plastic lever in the door. It requires a rhythmic, circular motion of my arm. I feel the mechanical resistance of the glass sliding into the metal frame. Analog. Physical. Direct.

The ignition key is a simple, notched piece of metal. When I turn it, the vibration travels through the gear knob in my palm and the soles of my boots. The sound of a transition.

I shift into gear. The mechanical clack as it locks into place.

The driveway is the boundary between the house and the horizon. The Michigan air is sharp and damp. The place where I stand between the life I built and the life I want.

I pull out onto the street.

The compound is a disappearing speck in my mirror.

Ahead of me is a road that doesn't require a badge or a password.

The rhythmic hum of the tires on asphalt. The music of an open-ended adventure.

No idea where I'm going.

No idea what's next.

ABOUT THE AUTHOR

Tom grew up in Detroit, Michigan, the kid who fixed things that weren't supposed to be fixable and found loopholes in every system he encountered. He spent over twenty years in corporate IT infrastructure before walking away in 2025. He's officiated roller derby, hung from silks twenty feet in the air, and built vans in his driveway. This is his first book.

FOR SPEAKING ENGAGEMENTS
AND MORE INFORMATION, VISIT
HTTPS://TOMKUSCH.COM/

ACKNOWLEDGMENTS

To everyone who told me to write a book within a few minutes of meeting me: this was for you. You saw something I couldn't see yet.

To my family and friends who stuck around even when I was figuring out who I actually was. To the ski club, the acting and improv community, the maker spaces where I built things that weren't supposed to work.

To the roller derby community: my chosen family. To the aerial circus crew who made me stronger in ways I didn't expect. To the farm people who welcomed me whether I had answers or not.

To the Police Auxiliary and Community Emergency Response Team volunteers I served alongside. To the Native American tribes who shared their wisdom and welcomed me.

To every corporate job and every coworker who watched me try to fit into boxes that weren't my shape. You were part of the journey even when it didn't feel like it.

To roommates and strangers and everyone who's ever built something with their hands in a driveway or driven toward an unknown destination just to see what happens. You made this journey feel less lonely.

To the people who let me tell their stories alongside mine. I changed some details to protect your privacy, but you know who you are.

And to anyone who's ever felt like they didn't fit the script they were handed: this one's for you.

www.ingramcontent.com/pod-product-compliance
Lightning Source LLC
Chambersburg PA
CBHW031957150726
47990CB00005B/1744